African Pastor-Teachers

Brief History of United Methodist Evangelism in Zimbabwe

A Study of the Role Played by the African Pastor–Teachers in Evangelizing their People and Planting churches in the Eastern and Northeastern Regions of Zimbabwe 1901-1921

by

Dr. John Wesley Zwomunondiita Kurewa

Africa Ministry Series

DISCIPLESHIP RESOURCES
— INTERNATIONAL —

African Pastor-Teachers

A Brief History of United Methodist Evangelism in Zimbabwe

Cover and interior design: Karin Wizer
Cover photo: Stock Image
Typesetting: PerfecType, Nashville, TN

ISBN 978-0-88177-871-7

Contents

Abbreviations

MECAMC: Minutes of the East Central Africa Mission Conference (1901–1925)

MRMC: Minutes of the Rhodesia Mission Conference (1917–1925)

JECAMC: Journal of the East Central Africa Mission Conference of the Methodist Episcopal Church (1901–1912)

Preface

Many Christians in Africa assume that Christianity was brought to Africa entirely by European and American missionaries. Often, missionary writers, including their historiographers, have promoted their publications on assumption that missionaries were the only primary actors in the propagation of the gospel, including the planting of churches in villages and towns of Africa. For example, official journals of early mission conferences of the Methodist Episcopal Church, which is now The United Methodist Church in Zimbabwe, often attached names of missionaries to great events pertaining to the spread of the gospel and the founding of churches in the villages. When it came to early African church leaders, who also participated in the same historical events of propagating the gospel and planting churches, the missionaries chose to record them merely as numbers. For example, one would read about a male missionary and his wife exploring in a certain area or visiting an African chief, "accompanied by two or five native helpers." These incomplete records make it difficult to know who these first Africans who participated in the establishment of the Church were, and from whence they came.

The primary purpose of this written history of the early church in Africa was feedback to the missionaries' mother churches in Europe or North America. Whether in official journals or private correspondence, the goal was to inform the mother churches of the missionaries' activities and to solicit more funding. Thus, the missionary was the main actor and not necessarily the "native helper." That approach to documenting the history of the Church in Africa has given the wrong impression, failing to promote the role of the missionary churches and especially the role played by the emerging national leadership.

Some African Christians do not perceive it as significant that African native helpers in their own right participated in the origin and propagation of the new faith in the history of Christianity in Africa. They believe the introduction of the church was entirely a creation of missionaries, and therefore Africans have to keep learning from those who created and brought this institution to Africa. Hence, to this day change takes place in the churches in Africa only when the mother church in Europe or North America takes the initiative to make that change. For example, ecumenical cooperation by churches in Africa often is adapted as a replica of what is happening in the homeland of mother churches. This may include new ways of ministry or understanding theology. Not only are the written history and study texts of Christianity in Africa misleading; rather, they have also tended to create a spirit of dependency and an attitude of immaturity on the part of African Christians.

The thesis of this book is that though originally called "native helpers," African leaders were in the forefront of propagating the gospel and planting churches, especially in the villages. As a matter of fact, official journals of the Methodist Episcopal Church in Southern Rhodesia show that native helpers took greater responsibility of planting churches in the villages. Although missionary names alone are highlighted in official journals of the Methodist Episcopal Church in Southern Rhodesia, a careful examination of the same journals and some private correspondences of missionaries and the personnel of the missionary boards or societies reveal names that can be matched with some of the historical events where only numbers had been used.

How easily we African Christians forget that Christianity existed in Africa from the origin of its history and that it was brought to Africa first by Africans. In Acts, his account concerning the early church, Luke is clear that Egypt and Libya had representatives in Jerusalem on the day of Pentecost (Acts 2:10). In speaking about the people who were present at the great event of Pentecost, Chrysostom (c. 347–407), a notable biblical preacher of Antioch, in his Epiphany homily, says, "the Ethiopian also understood,"[1] implying that Ethiopians were present. The point is that Africans were participants in the propagation of the gospel right from the day of Pentecost and during the early decades of Christianity in Africa. Again, Luke informs us of the Ethiopian eunuch who was baptized by Philip and went on his way to Africa rejoicing in the Spirit (Acts 8:36–39). In commenting about the same Ethiopian eunuch, Irenaeus said that the Ethiopian eunuch "became a missionary among his people."[2]

Similarly, from the sixteenth century CE, African preachers were heavily involved in preaching and planting churches in the African villages. In showing the process of propagating the gospel and planting United Methodist churches in the villages and towns of the eastern and northeastern regions of Zimbabwe, the purpose of this book is threefold.

First, we will discover that the missionaries were the explorers and strategists of the missionary activities. They made the initial contacts with African chiefs, and often they identified places where they wanted to establish mission stations and churches. And they approached the government officials to legalize the establishment.

Second, we will see that it was the African preachers, or native helpers, who were the frontier people, leading the way into the rural areas that had not yet been evangelised. They were the preachers of the gospel, almost every day. They founded the local churches and taught their people to read and write. Unfortunately, we will never know the names of some of those gallant African preachers and educators, as their involvement was often indicated by their numbers or by the term *interpreters*. Increasingly, the same documents show that those African preachers who might have been overshadowed by the missionaries were actually the heralds of the good news to their people.

Third, I will show that the ministry of the church is more effective when it is allowed to emerge from the socio-cultural situation of the new community. As the people responded to the gospel of Jesus Christ and committed themselves, they needed to be equipped by the gospel as well as by the courage to become incarnate communities as the Spirit led the new believers in Christ.

The primary source materials for this book are the official journals of the East Central Africa Mission Conference (1901–15) and the Rhodesia Mission Conference (1916–30) of The United Methodist Church in Zimbabwe. These official journals are rich with information that needs to be made known to the whole church. Also, private correspondences between missionaries and the Mission Board personnel of home churches were found to be invaluable resource materials.

I am indebted to Andra Stevens who read the whole manuscript; my secretary, Lovejoy Nyamavhuvhu, for attending to all details of the manuscript; and to my wife, Gertrude, for patience and encouragement as I worked on this book.

John Wesley womunondiita Kurewa
The Kurewa Chair, and E. Stanley Jones Professor of Evangelism
Africa University, Faculty of Theology
Old Mutare
8 September 2009

PART ONE

HISTORICAL BACKGROUND

This part of the book will give us the historical beginning of The United Methodist Church from the United States to Africa, and especially the origin of The United Methodist Church in Zimbabwe. Chapters 1, 2, and 3 provide that historical background.

Chapter 1

Episcopal Methodism in Liberia

Methodism's interest in evangelizing Africa was aroused and led by Africa's freed slaves in and from North America. It all began with an African American:

> The Missionary Society of the Methodist Episcopal Church was inspired into being (1819) through John Stewart. This black man, the son of free and pious Baptists in Virginia, was converted through Methodist preaching at Marietta, Ohio, 1816. He at once through a black interpreter, "a fugitive slave and backslidden Methodist," evangelized the Wyandots [a red Indian ethnic group] and now sleeps his last sleep among his Indian brethren. Thus John Eliot's joint ministry for the red man and the black was repeated in the ministrations of this Negro unto his Indian fellow-sufferers. The Church was aroused by its dusky son, and by him led into missions.[3]

Long before the formation of the Missionary Society of the Methodist Church in the United States in 1819, missionary work by the Methodist Church had already been started among the slaves in America. While the majority of plantation owners were in favour of the enterprise, there was opposition from some individuals, and "sometimes severe restrictions as a result of state laws."[4] By 1844, there were 150,000 African Americans enrolled in the Methodist Church.[5] Originally, Methodists were slower to conduct missionary work among the Native Americans than might have been expected. Most Methodist preachers were frontiersmen who shared the popular attitude toward the Native Americans that they were enemies. Those Methodist preachers had so much trouble trying to reach the scattered cabins of the whites when Native Americans "were on the warpath that they had little heart for any attempt to evangelize their enemies."[6] James Montgomery was the first missionary to be sent by the Ohio Conference to work among the Wyandots in 1819. Missionary work had already begun among the Wyandots by John Stewart, an African American preacher. While Frederick Noble in the above mentioned quotation said John Stewart was converted in 1816, Umphrey Lee and William Sweet say he was converted in 1815.[7] However, the main point is that John Stewart's work among the Native Americans was an essential element towards arousing the Methodist Church in forming its Missionary Society in 1819.

Origins of Methodism in Liberia

Daniel Coker, the founder of the African Methodist Episcopal (AME) Church in America, was born of a white mother, Susan, and a slave father in Maryland. Both parents worked for the same master. Daniel absorbed the rudiments of an education and "in his youth ran away from his master to New York City."[8] In New York, Daniel Coker became a Methodist and was ordained a deacon by Asbury, having proved himself a powerful preacher. In 1801, Daniel moved to Baltimore where an elder in the Methodist Episcopal Church, Michael Coate, helped him in purchasing his freedom.[9] For a time Daniel worked as a schoolteacher, and it was in Baltimore as he attended church that he felt the pains of segregation in the life of the church.

As a minister of the African Methodist Episcopal Church, Coker embarked to Liberia "on a missionary service" in 1822.[10] Before landing in motherland Africa with other freed slaves who were to settle in Liberia, Coker organized those who were Methodists into a society. Thus

Coker's group landed in 1822, not only as freed slaves coming back to motherland Africa, but also with a new identity—the Methodist Society, or the first Methodist Episcopal Church in Liberia.

Those freed slaves, *and not white missionaries*, introduced the Methodist Episcopal Church to Africa. The first white Methodist missionary to come to Africa was Melville Cox, who arrived in Liberia on March 8, 1833. He assisted in the creation of the Liberian Mission Conference within the Methodist Episcopal Church. Cox died within four months of his arrival in Liberia, and on his deathbed proclaimed, "Though a thousand fell, Africa must not be surrendered."[11] Medical missionary Dr. Goheen, who arrived in Liberia in 1836, rendered significant Christian witness through his medical service. The Liberian Mission Conference, which originated through the efforts of freed slaves, became the Liberian Annual Conference of the Methodist Episcopal Church of the United States in 1868.[12] The Liberia Conference was administered from America, as it was part of the racially divided Black Central Conference system in the United States. Because of the connection with the Black Central Conference in the United States, the Liberian Methodist work was not reckoned as part of the Congo Mission Conference that emerged later and embraced the rest of the Methodist Episcopal Church missionary work in Africa up to 1900.

In 1858, Bishop Francis Burns, an African-American preacher from America became the first missionary bishop for Africa until his death in 1863.[13] His successor was Bishop John Roberts (1866–75).[14] Neither Bishop Burns nor Bishop Roberts resided in Africa.

The Congo Mission Conference

Methodist Episcopal Church missionary work outside Liberia was known as The Congo Mission Conference of the Methodist Episcopal Church. Bishop William Taylor (1821–1902) was directly connected with the origin of missionary work beyond the borders of Liberia. Taylor is said to have been one of the converts of Phoebe Palmer,[15] a laywoman of the Methodist Church who had become a renowned leader in the holiness movement in New York City.[16]

Taylor became an evangelist of worldwide repute, traveling on preaching campaigns and establishing self-supporting missions in South America, Australia, and India. He also traveled on evangelistic missions in the Cape Colony and Natal[17] in South Africa. Taylor established those missions alone, without the involvement of his Methodist General Mission Committee. And he used the money that he received from the holiness movement camp meetings to send out missionaries. Because he believed in the idea of self-supporting missions, he expected the missionaries that were sent out to such missions to be self-supporting. Those missionaries rarely received any salary or other gifts. Consequently, many of them suffered or even died for lack of good health care. In 1882, the General Mission Committee "denied the right of Taylor or any person other than its regular appointees to organize Northern Methodist churches outside the United States."[18] That action led to the closure of Taylor's missions in South America. Missionaries who had been sent there under his efforts were recalled. However, the General Mission Committee would not "dissolve the South India Conference, erected from Taylor's labors in 1880."[19]

Taylor accepted the status of a local preacher. When he appeared at the [Philadelphia] General Conference of 1884 as a lay delegate from South India,[20] he was elected the first resident missionary bishop for Africa. There were a number of factors that led to the election of William Taylor as the missionary bishop of the Methodist Episcopal Church in Africa. First, Taylor was already an evangelist of repute in the United States and was well known for his evangelistic-missionary work in South America, India, South Africa, and New Zealand. Second, according to Frederick Norwood, during the early years of Methodism in America, Methodism was deeply involved in the holiness movement. Thus, one "powerful factor in the election of William Taylor as missionary Bishop in 1884 was support from advocates of holiness."[21]

Third, Taylor is said to have been "impelled by the impact of his apostolic personality."[22] Actually, he is considered to have done "more than any other one man to effect the broad geographic spread of American Methodism."[23] Fourth, Bishop Taylor shared with the Chicago Congress on Africa the circumstances surrounding his election as a resident missionary bishop for Africa, when he said:

> Discussion by the General Conference of the Methodist Church in 1884 brought out so discouraging aspects of their work in Africa that the Conference, but for the shame of defeat, would have given up the field. The next thing was to find a man to take the responsibility and become a scapegoat to bear their reproach into the wilderness and probably die in the jungle. The Conference was willing to risk my life. I was thrust into the breach by a more than two-thirds vote without discussion. They said, "We will turn him loose and let him do as he likes." [24]

Bishop Taylor's missionary work in Africa was marked by a number of ideas and attempts to bring those ideas to fruition. Some were achieved, and others were not. Taylor is believed to have had a plan for planting a chain of mission stations across Africa from the west to the southeast as a way of preventing Islam's encroachment further south. In 1854, Livingstone had passed through Angola and prayed that the church might gain harvest in the region.[25] It happened that in an attempt for Taylor to achieve his goal of establishing a chain of missions across Africa, he landed in Angola on 20 March 1885, accompanied by forty-two missionaries—including men, women, and children from America. Seven stations were reported established in Angola.[26] In September of the same year, Bishop Taylor was in Lisbon, where he met the king of Portugal, and in Brussels, where he met the patron sovereign of the Congo, Leopold II.

Taylor's meeting with the king of Portugal in Lisbon in 1885 enabled him to establish missionary work in Portuguese East Africa, now Mozambique, though at a later date. Erwin Richards, formerly a missionary of the American Board of Foreign Missions that belonged to what we know today as the United Church of Christ, came to Mozambique where his board set up a mission station at Inhambane in 1880.[27] Because of linguistic, political, and climatic difficulties that the American Board of Foreign Missions faced in Inhambane, the board decided to relocate its work to Gazaland, in the eastern region of Zimbabwe. Richards was in Gazaland, Southern Rhodesia, at the royal village of Umoya muhla, when Umzila, king of Gazaland granted his official sanction for the initiation of the American Board of Foreign Missions on 10 October 1881.[28] In spite of how highly Erwin Richards speaks of Umzila, the king of Gazaland, he did not agree with his church board's plan to terminate work that had already been established at Inhambane. As a result, Richards was not prepared to leave Inhambane.

It happened that missionary Dr. John Goucher, who must have been deeply involved with the American Board of Foreign Missions, had a long discussion with Bishop Taylor leading to the latter being petitioned to take over the missionary work at Inhambane Mission—an offer that he accepted. On Christmas Eve of 1890, Erwin Richards, who had earlier expressed his opinion against the decision by his church to abandon work in Inhambane, decided to join the Methodists and was commissioned as the first Methodist missionary at Inhambane Mission.[29] The bishop had achieved his dream to establish a chain of missions across Africa.

The trip to Brussels enabled Taylor to establish eleven mission stations in the Congo.[30] In 1886, the Taylor Mission on the Congo was inaugurated. Fifty-eight missionaries were recruited for the task, and the project cost about US $200,000. The results were sad because by 1896 only five missionaries were at work.[31] Those missionaries suffered greatly for lack of financial support, and the majority of them died. Of the eight posts, or mission stations, that had been founded, only Banana Point and Vivi remained occupied stations. The Anne Taylor, a boat worth US $75,000 was sold in 1896 for $3,000. There was truth in the principle of self-support, and indeed the principle had to be applied. However, Bishop Taylor's critics felt the Methodist Episcopal Church was at fault in 1884, "not in its representative, but in permitting his method."[32]

Bishop Taylor believed that missions in Africa should be indigenous as well as self-supporting.[33] This idea can be tracked back to Henry Venn, who in 1854 spoke of "the aim of mission as being the calling into existence of self-governing, self-supporting, and self-propagating churches."[34] Following that approach to missions, Bishop Taylor opened many mission stations with missionaries who came as volunteers without plans of remuneration from home churches other than what they were able to raise from some churches and the holiness camp meetings. As already indicated, many missionaries suffered for lack of support, with others dying from inadequate health care.

Bishop Taylor also believed that civilizing the African people was part of the missionaries' work. For example, he is reported as saying that one of his Episcopal responsibilities in Africa was "to embrace the industries necessary to the self-support of civilized life for all those whom we get saved and civilized."[35] He wrote about establishing a nursery in every mission station where children adopted from heathendom would be brought and nursed before they were old enough to become heathens themselves. Although some missionaries did not enthusiastically support the views of the bishop on this matter, they implemented the idea in a modified manner. For example, Erwin Richards, the first Methodist Episcopal Church missionary to Portuguese East Africa, shared this theory as it was being tried in Portuguese East Africa. Some missionaries raised African children in their homes or employed new converts to work in their gardens with the idea of separating them from their heathen home influences and training them in the new faith and new civilization in missionary homes.[36]

The theory behind all this was that as the converted and the home-trained children grew to maturity they would start homes of their own, and "live consistent Christian lives and shine as bright lights in the heathen world about them."[37] According to the missionaries who believed in that theory, the ultimate goal was to create "a little Christian community well worthy of the name of Church."[38] The theory failed to gain ground. Frederick Norwood says, "Probably, Taylor's greatest limitation was failure to understand the cultural environment in which he worked, sometimes like an American bull in an exotic china shop."[39]

In summary, The United Methodist Church in Africa needs to remind itself and celebrate the fact that it was Daniel Coker and other African freed slaves from America who introduced American Methodism to Africa when they landed as an organized Methodist Society in Liberia in 1882. Second, considering how deadly conditions in Africa were to the health of outsiders, it was providential that William Taylor—a man who was full of zeal to evangelize and establish mission stations on the continent—was elected as the first resident missionary bishop for Africa. Third, African Methodism should not lose sight of Bishop Taylor's idea that the Methodist Church in Africa needs to be "indigenous and self supporting." These words from the first resident missionary, bishop of the Methodist Episcopal Church in Africa, haunt all true and sincere United Methodists on the continent. It is only as we stand as United Methodists and Christians of Africa who assume the responsibility to support our evangelization programme that we make a meaningful contribution to worldwide Methodism and the rest of Christendom, as well as fulfilling the mission to which God has called us on this continent.

Chapter 2

Bishop on a Mission

Joseph Crane Hartzell (1842–1928) was responsible for opening Methodist Episcopal Church missionary work in Southern Rhodesia. He was elected resident missionary bishop for Africa in Cleveland, Ohio, in 1896, succeeding Bishop William Taylor, who had retired. For fourteen years Hartzell had "engaged in Negro work in the United States as a Corresponding Secretary of the Freedman's Aid and Southern Education Society."[40] That service prepared Hartzell for his Episcopal responsibilities in Africa.

Led by a Vision

Long before his election, Hartzell kept abreast of events on the African continent, carefully following the movements as the colonial nations scrambled for the continent, including the Berlin Conference of 1844. British northward expansion from the Cape had hastily annexed Botswana by 1885,[41] and in particular, Hartzell was excited about that northward movement of the British flag from South Africa to the regions beyond the Limpopo River. Bishop Hartzell was admired by his missionary colleagues as having "the plans of a great Christian statesman."[42] He sensed correctly that Cecil Rhodes, who had found a great fortune in the diamond and gold mines of South Africa, was a pivotal force behind that northward movement of the British flag. Thus, the Bishop sought to tie that northward march of the British flag with the Methodist Episcopal Church missionary work.

This was the way that the vision came to Hartzell. A few weeks before the General Conference, Hartzell made a presentation on the

"Partitions of Africa" before "a literary club in Cincinnati."[43] He claimed that the outline of his presentation, whose main content must have been the map of the partitioning of Africa "was before my mental vision."[44] Thus:

> During the cheering which followed the announcement of my election as a missionary Bishop for Africa, at Cleveland, Ohio, in May 1896, and before I was invited to the platform, the following words were distinctly impressed upon my mind, "Somewhere in South Africa in the midst of the advancing waves of Anglo-Saxon civilization northward and under the British flag, American Methodism should have missionary work."[45]

Following his election in May 1896, Bishop Hartzell made his first episcopal visit to Liberia, Angola, and Congo. After his second visit to the same three countries in 1898, we have the following report about the bishop's impressions:

> He publicly and repeatedly stated, "The mission work of our church is not what it had been represented to be." From personal inspection of the Liberian missions he ascertained that the expenses of the mission station were far beyond anything anticipated: many missionaries had proved unfit: of eighty-eight persons sent ten years ago only twelve were in the field; of the fifty stations opened only twenty five were said to be occupied; out of the forty five thousand coffee trees planted scarcely fifteen thousand had been saved; and the coffee sold would not exceed two hundred dollars. Good Bishop Taylor's large plans had miscarried, and the self supporting missions among Liberian pagans, though impelled by the impact

> of his apostolic personality, had cost about one hundred thousand dollars and a zealot sacrifice of life.[46]

September 1897 found Bishop Hartzell in England where Mrs. Hartzell, who had just come from America, joined him. The bishop had the opportunity to have a breakfast conversation with Cecil Rhodes while in London. The bishop is reported to have asked Rhodes what his chief ambition was in life. Rhodes replied:

> My ambition is two-fold: (a) to do the greatest possible thing for barbaric humanity, and (b) to do all in my power to promote the unity of the English-speaking races of the world. When that unity is a fact, there will be no more war.[47]

After that meeting with Cecil Rhodes, Bishop and Mrs. Hartzell left London for Cape Town. In Cape Town, the bishop had another meeting with Cecil Rhodes and Rhodes invited the bishop and his wife to attend the celebration for the completion of the railroad from Cape Town to Bulawayo, southern Zimbabwe. The invitation was accepted and that enabled the bishop and his wife to enter Zimbabwe for the first time in October 1897, following which the couple also visited Kimberley, Johannesburg, Pretoria, and other places of interest in South Africa. After the visit to South Africa, Bishop and Mrs. Hartzell traveled by sea from Durban to Biera in Mozambique.

Although we do not know the specifics of the conversation between the bishop and Cecil Rhodes, we can speculate that it was about the transfer of Mutare town from one site to the other. Nothing could have fulfilled Bishop Hartzell's vision of establishing the Methodist Episcopal Church under the British flag better than to have Rhodes hand over the old site of Mutare for a mission station in Southern Rhodesia.

Upon leaving Beira for Mutare, ready to make their second entry into the country, Bishop and Mrs. Hartzell learned that heavy rains had washed away the newly built railroad in several places. Nevertheless, they managed to travel by rail to Macequece (now Villa Perry), a distance of about 280 kilometres from Beira, with African labourers carrying them over the washouts. Because the railroad from Villa Perry was still incomplete, Mrs. Hartzell remained in Villa Perry in a mud hotel. The bishop traveled alone the last forty kilometres to Mutare on a horse that had been loaned to him by the governor of Portuguese Southeast Africa. As the bishop approached Mutare, he must have been deeply impressed with what he saw, for he wrote:

> After a horseback ride of twenty-five miles through mud and rain and crossing swollen rivers, I caught my first sight of the Mutare valley. The view was from the mountain pass. The valley was 3300 feet above the level of the sea and the thriving village in the distance on which the sun was shining, with the mountains surrounding, made a picture of restful beauty. The words that thrilled me at Cleveland came again, and I said, "There, or somewhere near, is the place."[48]

On Friday, 10 December 1897, Bishop Hartzell arrived on horseback in Mutare. In words reminiscent of Paul in his letter to the Galatians (4:12–14), Bishop Hartzell described his wretched state and welcome as he entered the village of Mutare:

> I rode into Umtali a stranger, weary and hungry, soaked with rain and bespattered with mud; but if ever a Methodist preacher was led by God, I believe I was, in coming to Umtali.[49]

Bishop Hartzell discovered that the new village of Mutare already had several European settlers. Mutare looked beautiful and healthy to the bishop, as its altitude was favourably high. He was further pleased by the great wave of migration of Europeans into the region under the protection of the British flag. The only church that he found in the new village was the Anglican Church. Through the combination of all these factors, Bishop Hartzell became convinced that "Here is the place for a great central mission among Europeans and natives."[50] On Sunday, 12 December 1897, the bishop conducted two services in Mutare. The first was held in the morning in a large office of a Dutch trading store and was attended by a number of Europeans. A request to secure some hymn books from a missionary of the Church of England was turned down, so the group had to settle on old familiar hymns that they could sing from memory.[51] The second worship service was held that same evening in a room of a company building that belonged to Messers. Wm. Phillipi & Co. (which later became the workshop of Puzey and Payne—a well known location in Mutare).

The Vision Unfolds

Bishop Hartzell began formal negotiations with the British South Africa Company toward the establishment of a mission centre at the abandoned site of Mutare. In doing so, the bishop dealt mainly with three persons—the administrator of Mutare, Captain Turner, the administrator of Rhodesia, Earl Grey, and Cecil Rhodes himself, who owned the British South Africa Company. On 21 March 1898, Bishop Hartzell received a letter from Earl Grey saying his request had been granted. He was to receive the old site of Mutare, which had thirteen thousand acres of land and several buildings. That site became known as Old Mutare Mission.[52] In addition, the Methodist Episcopal Church received seven lots, by 1913 valued at $6,000 to $8,000. On one of the lots to this day stands St. Andrew's Church, which was meant from the beginning to be for whites. In Penhalonga, the church received two lots, by 1913 valued at $2,000, and on one of the lots was St. Paul's Church, which was again a white congregation, and had cost $4,000 to erect.[53]

Adding all these gifts together, Bishop Hartzell speculated that they made the largest single donation ever received by the Methodist Episcopal Church in any foreign country.[54] There were conditions placed upon the donations though, namely: (a) that the Methodist Episcopal Church establish a school for European children in Mutare; and (b) that the same Church establish an industrial mission for the African children at Old Mutare Mission.[55]

Old Mutare Mission officially opened on 7 October 1898. On that occasion Bishop Hartzell preached on the text, "Fear not little flock, for it is your Father's good pleasure to give you the Kingdom" (Luke 12:32). Bishop William Taylor was an evangelist and a bishop with an apostolic personality. Bishop Hartzell was an accomplished leader and an ambassador of Christ who moved with confidence in the One whom he represented, in all the corridors of power for the sake of the kingdom of God.

We often hear of Hartzell's vision in conjunction with climbing Chiremba Mountain. I quote what the bishop himself recorded:

> Overlooking Old Umtali Mission Park is a mountain fifteen hundred feet higher than the plain where that audience lay prostrate in prayer to God. In 1899, after the papers for the land had been signed and words of cheer had come from the home Church, I climbed to the top of that mountain and alone kneeled before my Lord and poured out my soul in a prayer of thanksgiving and praise and then by faith claimed a new spiritual empire in Africa for American Methodism.[56]

Oral tradition about Hartzell's mountain-top experience goes on to say that the bishop had a vision in which he saw several young people—boys and girls—coming from different directions into the Old Mutare Valley, speaking in different languages. As already quoted above, the vision was "Somewhere in South Africa in the midst of the advancing waves of Anglo-Saxon civilization northward and under the British flag, American Methodism should have missionary work."[57] The vision to evangelize those African countries that were to come under the British flag in the northward movement of British colonialism seemed the original vision of Hartzell. The vision was unfolding itself. That vision seemed to begin unfolding with the introduction of the Central Training School that consisted of Theology, Literary and Normal, and Industrial Departments at Old Mutare Mission in 1919. The educational programme drew students not only from Southern Rhodesia, but also from Portuguese East Africa, Northern Rhodesia, Nyasaland, and Belgian Congo. Several young men and women came to Old Mutare to train as pastors, teachers, bricklayers, and carpenters. Equally significant, the teachers and instructors came from all those countries, including South Africa.

That the vision continues to unfold is evident in the establishment of Africa University in 1992. In this short time, Africa University has already made its name on the continent as an educational institution of higher learning, consisting of six academic units: Agriculture and Natural Resources, Education, Health Sciences, Humanities and Social Sciences, Management and Administration, Theology, and an Institute of Peace, Leadership and Governance. In the past few years, the university has attracted an average enrollment of 1,300 students from over twenty African countries annually. This phenomenal growth and diversity of student enrollment, including staff appointments, is not only a fulfillment of Bishop Hartzell's vision, but also of the university's mission, which is "to provide higher education of high quality, to nurture students in Christian values, and to help the nations of Africa achieve their national goals."

Chapter 3

Creation of the East Central Africa Mission Conference

Although the Methodist Episcopal Church work in Liberia began in 1822, the Liberia Annual Conference was not organized until 1834, and the annual conference was not given full status in the Methodist Episcopal Church in America with representation in the General Conference until 1968.[58] Also, the Liberia Annual Conference remained under the black Central Jurisdiction in America until 1964.[59] Bishop William Taylor's election to the episcopacy for Africa (1884–96) is credited with the creation of the Congo Mission Conference. The Congo Mission Conference consisted of all Methodist Episcopal Church work outside Liberia in Africa. As an evangelist, William Taylor preached in the British colonies of the Cape and Natal, and as bishop, he then supervised Methodist Episcopal Church missionary work in Liberia and where he founded and inherited missions, such as Congo, Angola, and Portuguese East Africa. Thus, it was Methodist Episcopal Church missionary work that he founded outside Liberia that was reckoned by the General Conference as the Congo Mission Conference.

In May 1900, the General Conference of the Methodist Episcopal Church, which met in Chicago, took the following action in regard to the Congo Mission Conference:

> In the case of the Congo Mission Conference it shall be divided into two Mission Conferences as follows: (1) The East Central Africa Mission Conference shall include the work in East Africa south of the equator. (2) The West

> Central Africa Mission Conference shall include the work in West Africa south of the equator. (Disc., 1900, p. 260).[60]

In accordance with the action of the General Conference, the East Central Africa Mission Conference was convened at the call of Bishop Hartzell and held its first session at St. Andrew, then the chapel of the Mutare Academy in Mutare, 16–25 November 1901.[61] The Bishop opened the session by reading two scripture texts: Isaiah 35 and Acts 2:1–15. Following the reading of scriptures, they all sang the hymn, "The Church's One Foundation Is Jesus Christ Her Lord. The bishop is said to have "led in a most earnest prayer."[62]

The First Episcopal Address

The first episcopal address of Hartzell to the first session of the East Central Africa Mission Conference consisted of tales of the remarkable accomplishments of the Methodist Episcopal Church work in both Portuguese East Africa and Southern Rhodesia. It was concerned as well with generating great expectations and hope for the future in the minds of the conference attendants. The speech included the following major issues: (a) the vision of establishing the Methodist Episcopal Church under the British flag, a vision that the bishop had perceived as the bishop-elect at the General Conference in Cleveland in 1896; (b) his nine-month episcopal visit to Liberia, Congo, and Angola, and his returning to England, where he was reunited with Mrs. Hartzell in September 1897, and their embarkment to Zimbabwe; (c) the arrival of Bishop Hartzell in Mutare on Friday, 10 December 1897, and (d) the consultations with Captain H. S. Turner, administrator of Mutare, Earl Grey, administrator of Rhodesia, and Cecil Rhodes, leading to the takeover of the old site of Mutare (Old Mutare) in a letter dated 21 March 1898.[63] The bishop interpreted the success of that great event of launching the new mission conference in the southern region of Africa to be a result of a combination of his episcopal efforts, the missionary society efforts, and the efforts of all missionaries who had responded promptly to the call and were already in the field.[64]

Organizing the Mission Conference

As the session commenced, Bishop Hartzell stated that by action of the General Conference all members of the Congo Mission Conference engaged in missionary work in East Africa south of the equator had automatically become members of the East Central Africa Mission Conference. At that time, the missionary work in East Africa south of the equator included work in Portuguese East Africa and Southern Rhodesia. The missionary members who already laboured under the Congo Mission Conference and now became members of the East Central Africa Mission Conference were:

Erwin H. Richards, an elder in full connection (Inhambane District, in Portuguese East Africa)

Morris W. Ehnes, a probationer (Mutare District)

James L. DeWitt, a probationer (Mutare District)

Three members were received by transfer from sister annual conferences of the Methodist Episcopal Church in the United States, namely:

Robert Wodehouse, from Texas Conference, probationer (Southern Rhodesia)

Frank D. Wolf, from Cleveland, Ohio, on trial (Portuguese East Africa)

John M. Springer from Chicago, Illinois, on trial (Southern Rhodesia)

The following lay missionary workers were also present and were invited to participate in the discussions:

Eddy Horace Greeley

George M. Odlum

Herman Heinkel

Mrs. J. L. DeWitt

Miss Harriette E. Johnstone

Mrs. Helen E. Rasmussen

Mrs. E. H. Richards

Mrs. R. Wodehouse

Mrs. F. D. Wolf, M.D.

Only two African representatives are recorded to have been present at the creation of the first mission conference in the region. One was Tizore M. Navess, an African pastor of the Makodweni Church in the Inhambane District.[65] Navess is recorded as pastor of the Makodweni Episcopal Church. The other was George Muponda, a layman and teacher at the Mutare African Methodist Episcopal Church. The Mutare African Church congregation as we shall see developed into what we know today as Hilltop United Methodist Church in Sakubva. Muponda also served as an interpreter at church for missionaries. He had received his education at Lovedale Mission in South Africa.[66] Two districts of the new conference were created, Inhambane District in Portuguese East Africa and Mutare District in Southern Rhodesia. Although the African pastor-teachers are our focus in this book, it is equally essential to note the announcement of the first appointments of the conference. They were as follows:

Inhambane District

(a) Gikuki and two out-stations: Erwin H. Richards and Mrs. E. H. Richards; African teachers: Farangwani and Matewu
(b) Kambini and two out-stations: Frank D. Wolf and Mrs. F. D Wolf; African teachers: Muti Sikobeli, Engilazi and Kaliji
(c) Makodweni and two out-stations: African teachers: Tizore Navess, Josiah Hayes, and Xinzabani Hayes
(d) Mission Press: Erwin Richards, and an African Printer, Gigalamugyo

Mutare District

(a) Mutare, St. Andrew Methodist Episcopal Church: Robert Wodehouse, pastor

(b) Academy: Principal R. Emory Beetham, Mrs. H. Tullock, and Miss Harriette E. Johnstone

(c) African Teachers: Charles Yafele, who was the first pastor of the Mutare Methodist Episcopal Church for the Africans.

(d) Old Mutare Industrial Mission: John M. Springer was the pastor; George M. Odlam was responsible for agriculture and the experimental farm, and was assisted by Herman Heinkel; and Eddy H. Greeley was a teacher and a botanist. Greeley was responsible for the opening of the boys' school at Old Mutare in 1901. Mrs. E. H. Greeley was the matron, and was supported by Mrs. Helen E. Rasmussen. The following missionaries were in America during the time of the conference: Morris W. Ehnes, Mrs. M. W. Ehnes, J. L. DeWitt and Mrs. J. L. DeWitt.[67]

On a lighter note, James Dewitt of the Mechanical Department of Old Mutare Industrial Mission presented a gavel to Bishop Hartzell. The gavel was made of the wood of a gun taken from Africans during the Matabele Revolt in 1896. In accepting the gavel, the bishop spoke of the appropriateness of the gift at the time of the first session of the East Central Mission Conference, and expressed the hope that the memento would be used by officers presiding in succeeding sessions.

Mark of a Methodist

According to John Wesley, the character or mark of a Methodist was not to be found in the opinions or phrases one used or by actions and customs or by stressing religion on any single part of it.[68] Rather "a Methodist is one who has 'the love of God shed abroad in his heart by the Holy Ghost given unto him'. . ."[69] Because a Methodist knows that he or she is saved through faith and by the grace of God, he or she cannot be quiet about what happened in his or her life. He or she becomes a living testimony. Like the man who was once blind, he or she will say,

"One thing I do know. I was blind but now I see!" That kind of testimony cannot be suppressed. That is what John Wesley describes as a mark of a Christian of the Wesleyan tradition, and indeed, all Christians who worship "the Father in spirit and truth" know it.

The piety to share testimony of what God is doing in one's life is typical of Zimbabwean United Methodists to this day. It can be traced back to the first session of the East Central Africa Mission Conference. On the second day of that session, 17 November 1901, Bishop Hartzell led the "Love-feast" worship service at St. Andrew's Methodist Episcopal Church, where participants shared testimonies. Most of the participants were missionaries, and about sixteen of them gave testimonies concerning their conversion, preparation, and appointment to the mission field.[70] In their conversion testimonies they all claimed Jesus Christ as the Saviour and Lord of their life. The reader may be interested in testimonies by two missionaries, Mrs. Wolf, a medical doctor, and Robert Wodehouse, a minister of religion. First, let us listen to the testimony of Mrs. F. D. Wolf:

> Missions and heathen are two of the words which I remember hearing in my youngest days. For the heathen were often spoken of, and my relation to them was early impressed upon my mind. I am sure I would have been converted long before I was for often when under conviction and about willing to surrender myself, the thought would come to me perhaps you will have to do something you are not willing to do, the foremost fear being the Foreign Mission field.
>
> After my conversion at the age of thirteen, I loved to hear and read of mission work, but would not attend a missionary meeting if I had even the merest excuse for remaining away and even if I did attend I would not take part in the services not even to help sing.

For several years I took part in Sunday school work and in the Young Peoples Society, but only in a half-hearted way, paying my missionary money regularly, and trying to persuade myself that that was all that was necessary, also trying to believe that there were plenty of heathen in Cleveland among whom I could work.

During my High School course, Rev. and Mrs. Woodsides, then on their way to Africa, spent several days at our home. Their conversation at the time and especially his prayer the evening of his departure when he earnestly prayed that God would make one of our family willing to go to the foreign field, impressed and worried me greatly. From that time, no matter what I was doing up to the time that I surrendered my all to God, his words kept ringing in my ears. While attending Medical College many an opportunity presented itself for doing good among the outdoor patients of the Dispensary. During my senior year I had the privilege of working in the Women's and Children's Dispensary where much good could be done. While in this work I tried to believe that that was all I was called to do, but still that voice within kept saying, "There is a greater work to be done." After my graduation from the Cleveland University of Medicine and Surgery in 1896, and the Post Graduate Medical College of New York in 1897, I became interested in a mission among the Polish Catholics outside of the City. Still that voice within was not quieted for it seemed as if it was rather disturbing me more and more for every book, paper, or even Medical Journal I picked up seemed to have something in regard to the call for missionaries, and it was not until after a great struggle with self in the fall of 1899 that I surrendered, and was willing to say:

"I'll go where you want me to go, Dear Lord,
O'er mountain or plain or sea:
I'll say what you want me to say, Dear Lord,
I'll do what you want me to do."

My desire was to go to India, but the call came from Africa. Therefore on September 11th of this year my husband and I sailed from New York on the SS Philadelphia, arriving in Umtali October 25th, in time to attend the conference.[71]

The second testimony is that of Robert Wodehouse:

It was at a Methodist revival meeting in Grahamstown, South Africa, that I found Christ when a lad of sixteen; I with some companions went forward to the penitent form; we did not find peace there, but went out into the Bush to pray, and before we returned that night we settled the matter and accepted Christ. My first impulse was to tell others of my new-found joy. I had opportunity occasionally in giving an address in the Sunday school of which I was a member. I was encouraged by the ministers to go on in the good work, and was given an occasional appointment in the country chapels. My name was placed on the plan as a Local Preacher on trial, and having passed the usual term and examinations, I became a fully accredited local preacher in year 1876. My life was a very busy one, preaching every Sunday in the native and English churches. The Lord was pleased to give me fruit and put His seal on the work. I felt the call of God to preach, and I could say like Paul, "Woe is me if I preach not the Gospel." In the year 1895, I went to America with my wife who was much broken in health. While in America I was offered the pastorate of a church at East Meadow, Long Island, which I accepted, and the Lord wonderfully blessed our work in giving us a gracious revival and enabling us to build a new church,

> which we felt entirely clear of debt. After a pastorate of five years we were led to offer ourselves for Mission work again in Africa under Bishop Hartzell, and were accepted for the white and native work in New Umtali. We left New York Jan. 4, 1901, on the steamship Minneapolis, for the East African field. We had prayed much about it, and believed it was God's appointment. Our journey out was a propitious one, and the ten days in London enabled us rest, after five years of almost incessant work. After a pleasant stay in London, we sailed for our destination in the Gcaleka; opportunities for service occurred on board, and God's blessing attended the services which were held, with the result of two cases of conversion, and the strengthening of a number of young men, who, at first were inclined to break away from all restraint. A noonday prayer meeting held by the ladies in the cabin was a source of great blessing to God's children. We experienced many delays after reaching Cape Town, and arrived in Umtali April the 4th.[72]

The bishop called upon two African leaders to also share their testimonies. Tizore Navess made an extempore.[73] Although his testimony is not recorded, it was reported that "among the things which he mentioned were the coming of the missionaries, his surprise and joy of learning of the possibility of unending life, his early interest in religion, and his sound conversion. He manifested remarkable strength of character and knowledge of the revealed Word. . ."[74] The second African was George Muponda, who "gave a statement of his conversion,"[75] and again, sadly, that statement was not recorded.

What that "love feast" did was to lay down the foundation of what the Methodist Episcopal Church become known for in Southern Rhodesia. Sharing of testimonies is a common character of United Methodists to this day. Nowadays, in a United Methodist Church we have found that a revival meeting would be considered incomplete without time for testimonies. There is a point where pastors and church leaders need to help other Christians in making a testimony. The point is that, if your sins have been covered, why do you want to uncover and talk about them again? The heart of the message of Christian testimony is that it is primarily sharing with others God's love shed for us, sharing the forgiveness that we did not deserve, and escaping the damnation that had long awaited us.

With that teaching, sharing testimonies is an important and rich mark of a United Methodist, and should never be discouraged. Terence Ranger, a renowned historian, professor of race relations and Chair of the Africa Studies Committee of Oxford University, made an interesting observation about African United Methodist testimonies. He said:

> African Christian testimonies—made use of and interpreted in all these ways—constituted a major genre of both official and popular Methodism in eastern Zimbabwe and Mozambique. Nothing similar survives for eastern Zimbabwean Catholicism and Anglicanism. AMEC [American Methodist Episcopal Church] missionaries not only had a particular interest in testimonies, they also had a particular interest in sermons.[76]

After the East Central Africa Mission Conference introduced a printing press at Old Mutare Mission in 1907, and following the 1918 Revival, a conference paper named *Umbowo* (Testimony or Witness) was introduced. One of the objectives of the paper was to convey and share Christian testimonies with both Christians and non-Christians. Thus, at the first session of the East Central Africa Mission Conference in Mutare, the Methodist Episcopal Church demonstrated one of its greatest marks by sharing, encouraging, and inspiring one another through the love-feast of testimonies.

PART TWO

EVANGELIZATION OF CENTRES AND FRONTIERS

At the second session of the East Central Africa Mission Conference held at Mutare in 1903, two issues stood out prominently as recorded in the Report of Resolutions. First, the report cited the success and progress of work since the previous conference session of 1901. This included the rise of church membership, the splendid church building of St. Andrew's Methodist Episcopal Church and the Mutare Academy, and the growing strength of Old Mutare Industrial Mission that gave Methodist work prominence in the country. Second, numerous requests continued coming from African chiefs for teachers and evangelists to open schools, evangelize the villages, and take care of the health of the people. In response, missionaries themselves talked of the recruitment of more missionaries to the field. It was all these issues that led Bishop Hartzell to suggest that the delegates take one evening during that second conference session to share what was going on and possibly come up with a strategy for the evangelization of the African villages.[77] The bishop is quoted as saying:

> Africa is in the eye and getting more and more into the heart of the Christian Church... My great ambition is to get another large concession of land a thousand miles north from here. Civilization is rapidly moving northward, and we must begin our work and hold the place until we occupy it fully.[78]

The bishop is said to have concluded the discussion that evening by challenging his audience with the question "What have we done and what are we going to do?"[79] The general response by some missionaries to the bishop's challenge was to recruit more missionaries, even as many as "fifteen more missionaries and wives."[80] However, a few years later other missionaries, such as John Gates and A. Butcher, expressed a different view. John Gates said:

> There is no question in this Conference today that reaches the magnitude of this one. The evangelization of this race, as of all others, depends upon the native himself. The work of God in this land is strengthened or made weak according to the life and spirit of the native evangelist.[81]

Gates did not utter those words merely as a matter of policy or stating a theory; rather he was also saying what he was observing in the evangelistic task of the church in his time. Similarly, A. L. Buchwalter, Gates's contemporary, had this to say, although his statement was to some extent patronizing:

> I am glad to look upon these native teachers as a band of noble men, they and their kind are always the real backbone and strength of the work, for I think it is now conceded that the way to evangelize any people is through a native ministry. I have talked to these men and questioned them about their personal experiences and the work they are doing. I believe they are earnest godly men, that they love the Lord and are glad to tell the story of full salvation, as they know it.[82]

Chapters 4, 5, and 6 show us how the African pastor-teachers were involved in evangelizing their own people and planting churches, schools, and clinics and hospitals in the villages, towns, and missions.

Chapter 4

Evangelization of Mutare and Its Frontier

Not long ago, Mutare District embraced the circuits in Mutare itself, and the chieftainship areas south of Mutare that included Zimunya, Mutambara, and Marange. For the purpose of discussing the evangelization of this frontier of Mutare, we shall add Penhalonga. This makes sense as you might have noted in the introductory statement for Part Two. Thus we shall discuss them in the following order: Mutare, Pemhalonga, Zimunya area, Mutambara area, and Marange area.

The Mutare African Church

We already noted that Bishop Hartzell dedicated the first church building in the history of Episcopal Methodism in Zimbabwe and in Mutare—the Mutare African church. That event took place during the first session of the East Central Africa Mission Conference, and it marked the Mutare African Church as the mother church of Episcopal Methodism in Zimbabwe. The first church building was constructed of pole and mud, and was situated at the corner of Second Street and East Avenue. In 1905, the pole and mud building was replaced by a brick church building that was unfortunately blown down by a whirlwind in 1912. With the implementation of the Land Apportionment Act (1931), which was a demand by white Rhodesian farmers for the separation of white and black land, the African congregation was moved from what had become white land to a hilltop in Sakubva Township[83] where the congregation is now known as the Hilltop United Methodist Church, with a membership of about three thousand people. Charles

Yafele was the first "native helper," appointed as pastor at the Mutare African Church in 1901. Originally from South Africa, his evangelistic work in that church was reported as extremely encouraging. The figure of two hundred converts by 1903 was considered conservative.[84]

During the course of the same year, David Ntuli, another South African preacher, was also appointed to the Mutare Church to assist with both pastoral and teaching responsibilities.[85] In addition, new work opened up at the Location (African Township), now commonly known as "The Old Location." Wodehouse claimed to have built the new school-church building with his own hands in the Old Location, but with the assistance Charles Yafele. Regular Sunday services and a day school for children had already begun by 1905.[86] In the same year Charles Yafele was replaced by William Yafele as pastor and teacher. Despite all those changes, conversions were continually occurring at the Mutare African Church. It was remarkable that those conversions occurred during the regular Sunday worship services[87] of the Mutare Church rather than in specially arranged revival meetings. In the same year, 1905, John Malgas, another South African coloured preacher, was appointed as pastor and teacher at the Mutare Church. Malgas is reported to have been a zealous and faithful preacher,[88] who had an outstanding ministry in Mutare. As conversions occurred nearly every Sunday, the congregation soon had need for a larger church building.

One is likely to ask why there were so many preachers from South Africa coming to work in the Methodist Episcopal Church in Southern Rhodesia. Although we have not found a definitive answer, we can speculate that South Africa had well established mission stations that provided education for the Africans, such as Lovedale, a Presbyterian mission that drew students from South Africa and the surrounding countries. It was already noted that George Muponda, a teacher and an interpreter in Mutare, had received his education at Lovedale. In addition, before his election to the episcopacy, Bishop Taylor had held evangelistic campaigns in both the Cape and Natal Provinces. Bishop

Hartzell also went through South Africa on his trip from Bulawayo to Durban, where he and his wife got on a boat to Beira in order to enter Southern Rhodesia through Mutare. Another factor is that Robert Wodehouse, who received Christ at the age of fifteen years at a Methodist revival meeting in Grahamstown, South Africa, was one of the earliest missionaries to arrive in Mutare on 4 April 1901. The coming of the South African Methodist preachers to work in the Methodist Episcopal Church in Southern Rhodesia at that time may have been due to connections by some of the above mentioned leaders.

A remarkable thing about the Mutare Church is that they became conscious of the fact that they were the mother church, and by 1907 they had sent out not less than five hundred members of that church to share the gospel with others.[89] They sent some of the younger men to train at Old Mutare Mission, and they already had eight African preachers in the Mutare district. They were proud of having some of the best young leaders in the conference.[90] Unfortunately, John Malgas's ministry at the Mutare Church was short-lived because of his untimely death. In 1909, he uttered the following words on his deathbed as a living testimony:

> My end has come. Soon I am going above where God is. I want to leave this testimony that it may be told to my brothers. God called me to the work of preaching the Gospel. My work is now finished. My soul is in peace and my heart is washed in the blood of the Lamb. I have nothing against any man. I was glad to preach the Gospel. Now my end has come and God is with me and I am very happy. I have seen the heavenly Temple. There were no doors. I saw many people. They were of all colours. Each had an open book in his hand. Although there were so many yet the house was not full. It was God's Temple, the home he has prepared for me.[91]

As the Mutare church could not contain the evangelistic spirit within itself, its members looked outwardly. Thus, the Mutare Church evangelistic spirit became contagious as it spread southward.

Zimunya Area

Muradzikwa is located about twenty kilometres south of Mutare, in Chief Zimunya's area. In 1905, David Ntuli was appointed to spearhead and take charge of the evangelistic work of establishing the Methodist Episcopal Church at Muradzikwa. Together with his people, Chief Zimunya took a personal interest in assisting David Ntuli with the erection of the church building at Muradzikwa. Wodehouse, the presiding elder of Mutare, reported at the 1905 Mission Conference session that already forty conversions had occurred at Muradzikwa Church, with nearly one hundred children enrolled in school.[92] Ntuli had also visited villages in the vicinity, and he seemed to have had a plan to continue with his pastoral visits to all the surrounding villages. Immediately, there was great response to the evangelistic work in the whole area. Needless to say, evangelistic work, with the Mutare Church as the base from which to propagate the gospel, spread like wildfire. It was like the experience of the early church as reported in the first few chapters of the Book of Acts. That evangelistic thrust led to the founding of churches in both Zimunya and Marange areas. It was reported at the 1905 Conference that there were already "fifteen stations in connection with our native work in this circuit, which are being worked and having the Gospel preached to them regularly."[93] Credit was given to Charles Yafele, David Ntuli, and the seven unnamed exhorters who all preached under the demonstration and power of the Holy Spirit.[94]

Although we are not told who first brought the good news at Munyarari, which is about twenty kilometres south of Muradzikwa, by 1909 Wodehouse reported that there had been many conversions among the people at Munyarari, "among them several witch doctors, who have sent their charms and all the paraphernalia connected with their superstitious rites into Mutare."[95] What we gather is that by 1909, Gezana Sadomba was the pastor-teacher at Munyarari. He could have been the man behind the wonderful evangelistic work that was reported by Wodehouse.

Penhalonga Mining Village

Penhalonga was the first settlement of the white population in the eastern highlands. The first whites to settle in the village were Portuguese, from whom the name came. Penhalonga is said to mean "a village in the valley." Later on, the Portuguese were pushed out by British settlers, who later moved to what we now know as Old Mutare, and again, moved to the present Mutare location in 1895, following the railway road connection between Salisbury and Beira. Penhalonga's attraction has always been its gold. To this day, it is a significant gold-mining village in the eastern highlands.

As early as 1905, there were about two thousand African employees in the two mines of Penhalonga. Those African employees came primarily from Zimbabwe, Mozambique, and Malawi. The majority of the men left their wives in their village of origin, because housing and salaries for African employees in those days did not make provision for a wife. In spite of the official arrangements, some of the men brought their wives to Penhalonga, either for the duration of their employment or periodically. Many more women came to co-habit with willing male employees. Consequently, by the time the mines of Penhalonga were shut down temporarily in the 1950s, the village had a reputation as a place of prostitution.

Evangelistic work of Methodist Episcopal Church in Penhalonga began in 1905. Mr. Baker, the manager and engineer of the mines in Penhalonga, reportedly was a Christian who was sympathetic to the Methodist Episcopal Church missionary work. When the Methodist Episcopal Church wished to establish their presence in Penhalonga, permission was readily given.[96] Prior to the report to the Mission Conference session, regular worship services for a white congregation had begun, although without a pastor. In 1905, Charles Yafele moved from

Mutare to Penhalonga to spearhead the evangelistic work among the African workers and his wife served as a teacher for the gold-mining village. The concentration of about two thousand African employees from various African countries in Penhalonga presented one of the most challenging opportunities for evangelistic work to the church. The results were very encouraging. Fifty-nine conversions were reported at the gold-mining village by 1907, and two churches were built in Penhalonga—one in Penhalonga Compound with Charles Yafele as the pastor, and another at the Rezende Compound with James Viringa as the pastor.[97] The congregation at Penhalonga Compound had increased to twenty-three full members and 293 probationers.

Charles Yafele shared a miracle story at the 1909 conference. He had visited *Muzvare* (daughter or sister of a chief) Nyakuwanika, where he was challenged by the people:

> Where is the rain now we turned away from our gods and you say we must follow your living God and since that we cannot get any rain! We have made up our minds that if the rain does not come this week our children will not come to church any more.[98]

Charles Yafele responded:

> I at once called the people together for prayer asking God to send the rain and while we were praying God sent the rain. Praise God from whom all blessings flow, He saved us from being laughed at by the heathens.[99]

Mutambara Area

Mutambabra is situated about seventy-five kilometres south of Mutare, and was the second mission station to be established by Methodist Episcopal Church in Zimbabwe. Robert Wodehouse, the presiding elder of the Mutare area, reported the origin of Mutambara Mission to the 1905 Mission Conference session. Wodehouse, in the company of an African evangelist whose name he does not give, had visited Mutambara three times and had held a series of worship services each time. This series of services included preaching and Wodehouse needed an African evangelist either as an interpreter or a preacher. We can speculate that the African evangelist or pastor-teacher would have been Charles Yafele, David Ntuli, Stephen Tiki, or John Mazonya. Wodehouse went on to report that as a result of those visits, Chief Mutambara, having received consent from the government, gave a hearty invitation to open up a mission station in his area, which had a large population.[100] Wodehouse assured the conference that he was planning to construct a church building big enough for four hundred to five hundred people. He was impressed by the fertile land, which was well watered by two rivers at the proposed site of the mission station.[101]

At the 1905 Mission Conference, the bishop appointed Stephen Tiki to begin evangelistic work at Mutambara. In 1907, John Mazonya, who was the first African convert in Mutare under the ministry of Charles Yafele in 1901,[102] succeeded Tiki at Mutambabra. Although Wodehouse did not report much development at Mutambara, he shared that Mutambara was an important station and he had hoped to see it officially opened that year.[103] By the time of the 1908 session, which was actually held in November 1907, the presiding elder reported that nothing significant had been done at Mutambara, implying that no resident missionary had been sent to Mutambara. However, John Mazonya was still holding the fort as the evangelist.[104]

The first missionaries to be appointed to Mutambara Mission were A. L. Buchwalter and his wife, who arrived at their new appointment on 9 April 1908.[105] Unlike Old Mutare Mission, which had plenty of empty buildings when missionaries arrived, Mutambara had absolutely nothing for them to use. Speaking about his impressions and experiences after arriving at Mutambara, Buchwalter said:

> There was neither house nor familiar face to welcome us, a few strangers on the veldt that was all. Our goods were piled by the roadside in the tall grass, and we began mission work at the beginning.[106]

In spite of the negative impressions they experienced upon their arrival, as the Buchwalters got to know Chief Mutambara, they found him friendly and supportive of their work. The chief took an active part in sending young men to school, and encouraged people to attend Sunday services.[107] On the afternoon of the day they arrived at Mutambara, Mrs. Buchwalter began teaching a few girls in the door of their tent. One of the girls had the determination to learn the entire alphabet at one sitting. Fifteen months later, that girl was reported to have been able to read the New Testament in her language, and was also learning the English language.

In September 1908, an invitation was extended to those who wished to accept Christ as their Saviour and thirteen people came forward to the altar. By the time of the sixth session of the Mission Conference in July 1909, the number of persons who had made a public confession of their faith had risen to about seventy. Buchwalter and his wife visited a number of villages around Mutambara Mission. Buchwalter himself traveled as far as the border of Portuguese East Africa in the east, and Odzi River in the west. Still, Buchwalter interestingly pointed out that "The native evangelists have visited more extensively, but together we have not yet reached all of the people."[108] Again and again, these official documents of the church show us that the African evangelists, rather than the missionaries, were often in the forefront of propagating the Christian faith to their own people.

Later in 1909, Buchwalter gave credit for the propagation of the gospel to those Christian men living on the mission who had "rendered valuable assistance, visiting and preaching in the near by villages and some times going on a several days' preaching tour."[109] A man named

Verinisi was mentioned as an interpreter trained by missionaries for that job; and most likely, John Mazonya was still one of the two evangelists mentioned as two African helpers.[110]

On 12 May 1908, Edith Mae Bell left the Mutare Academy for Mutambara. The Buchwalters had already been taken away, presumably due to illness, and in January 1910, went to America. In assuming her teaching responsibilities, Bell was assisted by Aaron Kaloshe, who also had been assigned the responsibility to open an out station.[111] However, by 1910, Thomas O'Farrell, Edith Bell, and five African helpers were appointed at Mutambara Mission to carry on with the evangelistic work of the church and the educational task that included both boys' and girls' schools. Many other missionaries and African helpers joined later as the mission was established.

Marange Area

Wodehouse reported two trips that took several weeks down the banks of the Odzi River as far as the Sabi River. Although he uses the plural "we," we have no idea who accompanied him. We can only speculate that he was joined by at least one African evangelist, as was his practice. On one of the two trips, he went to Chief Marange's village that was situated on the top of Mount Makomwe.[112] After staying several days at the chief's place, an invitation was extended for the Methodist Episcopal Church to begin work there. At the foot of the mountain, the chief selected a site for the mission station. Bishop Hartzell appointed Eddy Greeley to work at Mount Makomwe in 1906.[113] During the same year, Wodehouse, Ferris, their spouses, Greeley, Chief Marange, and his counselors visited the site where the mission was to be established. Having been satisfied with the chief's selection and offer, four weeks later, Greeley, accompanied by four unnamed native helpers, "camped for three months under the trees, while the house was being built."[114] Greeley may have brought with him four young African men or students from Old Mutare Mission. Preaching of the gospel was launched in Chief Marange's area, and by the end of 1906 twenty converts had already been won to Christ.[115] Both a church and a school were established, and the number of students rose to forty-eight. English and Shona were taught from the beginning, and later on geography, English grammar, and arithmetic were added. For the first time, two of the elder native helpers are mentioned by name: Mandara Manjengwa and David Mandisodza. They are said to have helped with teaching and hymn writing.[116] In his report to the 1917 conference, Greeley disclosed the author of a hymn that had been a source of great inspiration to Methodists in Zimbabwe, Jonas Mandara Manjengwa. The author, from the Zimunya area, wrote to a tune typical of the African rhythm. The words go as follows:

Ndofamba, dofamba
Ndosuwa kudenga
Kunyika yaTenzi
Isina nenhamo

The other helper, David Mandisodza, came from Vumbunu in Mutasa area. At the 1908 conference, Mandisodza spoke for himself:

> When I came to the Mission I did not know how to read or interpret or preach or teach. So, Mr. Greeley taught me all these things and the Lord has been my helper too. When God sent me among the heathen I found them very cheeky. . .[117]

The Odzi farm, which consisted of 256 acres, was acquired in 1918 or 1919 with the intention that it would become the centre of the Marange Circuit.[118] The plan was to establish and develop a mission station at Odzi farm. Although Odzi was not near the concentration of the Marange population, the farm was close to the railway road and would have made traveling from Odzi to other places easier. Unfortunately, the goal was never fulfilled.

A significant development during the period of planting and establishing the Methodist Episcopal Church was the emergence of independent preachers—African preachers whom the Methodist missionaries found already preaching to their own people entirely at their own initiative. A notable example of these independent preachers is Johannes Chimene. Chimene, son of a chief in Zimbabwe, converted to Christianity while working in the mines in Transvaal, South Africa. Upon his return home to Masvingo, he began to preach the gospel to his people with great passion. In June 1906, when Robert Wodehouse and Eddy Greeley visited Masvingo area intending to open new stations, they found Johannes Chimene preaching the gospel of Christ. He joined the Methodist Episcopal Church at the invitation of Robert Wodehouse. In the report of the conference Committee on the State of the Church, the presiding elders speak of a 33.3 percent gain in church membership, including the tremendous evangelistic work that Johannes Chimene was doing in the Masvingo area.[119] At the 1909 conference, Johannes Chimene had this to say about his preaching:

> I have been preaching and praying with my people all the time. They are asking for the way now. The people are calling for the teachers. They say the darkness is great.[120]

Chapter 5

Evangelization of Old Mutare and Its Frontier

Old Mutare continues to tower majestically as the Jerusalem of United Methodism in Zimbabwe. With the establishment of Africa University on land that was part of the original mission station, Old Mutare has increasingly enhanced her status as a great centre of Christian influence. It was the first Methodist Episcopal Church mission station to be established on 21 March 1898, by the agreement between Bishop Hartzell of the Methodist Episcopal Church and the British South Africa Company. The historical background of the transfer of Old Mutare to the Methodist Episcopal Church is as follows. The first settlement of the white population in the eastern highlands of Southern Rhodesia was Penhalonga, which is a gold-mining village to this day. Later, the white population moved to Old Mutare, which was then Mutare. As the railroad was under construction from both Harare and Beira, it was found that a range of mountains lay between the railroad and Mutare. Consequently, Rhodes, who was the backbone of the British South Africa Company, ordered Mutare town, which still had a population of three hundred white people, to be moved to a site where the railroad could reach it. Thus in 1895, new Mutare was established about sixteen kilometres south of the old site, which was then known as Old Mutare.

The Origin of Old Mutare Mission

Following the negotiations between Bishop Hartzell and Rhodes, and the consultations among the concerned administrators with Rhodes, on 21 March 1898, Bishop Hartzell received a letter from Earl Grey, then Administrator of Rhodesia, "proposing concessions in lands and buildings in both New and Old Umtali for church and missionary work."[121] There were some conditions in the agreement upon which Old Mutare became the first mission station of the Methodist Episcopal Church in Southern Rhodesia including: (a) the establishment of a school for Europeans in New Mutare, and (b) the planting of a large and well equipped Industrial Mission for Africans at Old Mutare.[122] That agreement made the Methodist Episcopal Church a vital contributor toward laying the foundation of education, not only for Africans at Old Mutare but also for the population of the new white settlers in Mutare. The gift to the church included the village itself, with a significant number of buildings (some of which still stand to this day) and 13,000 acres of land.[123] Hence, Bishop Hartzell reported, "This is, perhaps the largest single gift ever made to our Church in a foreign land."[124] He went on:

> On my return to the United States in 1898, this great and providential opening for a new spiritual empire in East Africa was cordially recognised by the Bishops, Missionary Society, and Church at large.[125]

Old Mutare Mission officially opened on 7 October 1898. On that occasion Bishop Hartzell preached on the text, "Fear not little flock, for it is your Father's good pleasure to give you the kingdom" (Luke 12:32). The Old Mutare Mission Church is now known as Ehnes Memorial Church, named after Morris Ehnes, the first missionary along with his wife, on the new field in October 1898. Both Ehnes and his wife were graduates of Ohio Wesleyan University. Ehnes's first appointment was in Mutare, where he opened both school and church work among the Europeans.[126] Robert Wodehouse and his wife arrived to take over church work among both whites and blacks while Ehnes continued with school work until he returned to America in June 1901. In July of the same year, Reverend Emory R. Beetham, a graduate of Drew Theological Seminary, was appointed principal of the school in Mutare. Harriette E.

Johnstone of the State Normal School of New Jersey joined the school, making it possible to open two new departments—kindergarten and music. At the beginning of 1902, Rosa St. C. Tulloch joined the staff. On 13 December 1901, two important things happened for the school in Mutare: (a) the property the school then occupied was purchased for US $15,000, and (b) the school was named The Umtali Academy.[127]

It is important for the United Methodists in Zimbabwe to know that it was the Methodist Episcopal Church that established the Mutare Academy, which later developed into what is known as the Mutare Boys High. St. Andrew's was the chapel facility for the Academy. It is important to remember that The United Methodist Church has often been in partnership with government in providing education for young men and women in this country. However, the partnership at the Mutare Academy was short lived, for the Academy was passed on to government in 1909.[128] The transaction was to the mutual benefit of all involved.

The Reverend M. H. Reid was the first active missionary at Old Mutare Mission, having arrived with Morris Ehnes and his wife in October 1898. Reid was not a regularly appointed missionary, but was under the employment of the mission.[129] During the first rainy season after his arrival, he recorded and took care of the property at Old Mutare as the European settlers moved to the new site of Mutare. Since the police barracks were still at Old Mutare,[130] Reid provided pastoral care and conducted religious services each Sunday for the police until their move to New Umtali.[131] The three missionaries were soon to be joined by others, including James DeWitt and Mrs. DeWitt, both graduates of Ohio Wesleyan University; Mrs. Anna Arndt and her assistant, Herman Heinkel, who arrived at Old Mutare in April 1899; Eddy Greeley, who with his wife first worked in the West coast, where she died. Greeley arrived married to Anna Arndt, and took charge of the school at Old Mutare Mission. He enrolled twenty-seven boys. John M. Springer, a graduate of Northwestern University, arrived in June 1901, and took up work on the Industrial mission. And on 4 July George Odlum, a graduate of Michigan Agricultural College, arrived to take charge of the agricultural department. Helen E. Rasmussen, originally a worker in the Congo Mission, arrived and was to represent the Women's Foreign Missionary Society.[132]

The Industrial School at Old Mutare

Old Mutare Mission was founded with the primary purpose of establishing an industrial education centre. It was Greeley who started the boys' school at Old Mutare in 1901. The first male student at Old Mutare was Kaduku Nyamurowa, who unfortunately died while still a student and was buried at the missionary cemetery. By 1905, Helen Springer, who had been appointed to take charge of the Old Mutare general school in 1903, reported a breakthrough of five girls among seventy-six students who had been enrolled that year.[133] From that point, Old Mutare Mission developed in such a way that it became the most attractive mission centre of the Methodist Episcopal Church. Further, by 1919, the Central Training School that consisted of Theology, Literary and Normal, and Industrial Departments had been introduced at Old Mutare Mission.

The reader may be interested to note that at the beginning of 1901 the Eastern Rhodesia Experiment Station was established at Old Mutare Mission under the direction of Odlum with Greeley as the botanist. That experimental station conducted its work in cooperation with the Department of Agriculture of Southern Rhodesia.[134]

Second, from the beginning, Old Mutare Mission was a base for evangelistic thrust to the surrounding villages. Most requests from chiefs and villages for a teacher or evangelist were presented at Old Mutare.[135] Old Mutare Industrial School itself provided a challenging arena for both education and evangelism. By 1905 young men, young married couples,[136] and indeed, young girls[137] came to the mission for an education. The Industrial School evangelized through its educational programme, as the greater part of the curriculum was religious instruction. John Springer reported that in advanced classes two out of the three daily readings were in the Bible, and went on to make this point:

> We seek ever to keep before our minds that the primary object of the work is the revelation under the blessing of the Holy Spirit of God as the Father, and Christ as the personal Saviour of the soul.[138]

The study of the Bible was both in the vernacular and in English. One could easily say that education was used as a means to bring good news to the people because education itself was good news. By the end of 1905, Springer was boasting of having baptized ten persons who were actually residing in the mission. In the same year, Helen Springer reported the opening of the school for girls with five girls enrolled. She also stated the purpose of education to all who came to Old Mutare Industrial School, namely to give them the Bible and to enable them read it. The coming of the first five females at Old Mutare Mission was good news particularly to the missionaries, whose plan was to enable some of the young men who were soon to go out as teachers and evangelists to marry someone who had received education and training also.[139] In announcing their coming to Old Mutare, Helen Springer also mentioned that the five young women were already engaged to marry young men who were training to go out as teachers and evangelists. Those young women were studying the vernacular, writing, arithmetic, sewing, and housework.

Shirley Coffin was pastor in charge of Old Mutare Mission by 1907 and had "five native helpers" whose names are not disclosed.[140] Old Mutare Mission remained under the missionary pastors until 1936, when Josiah Chimbadzwa was appointed the first African pastor of the mission station.

The Surrounding Villages

When Old Mutare Mission opened in 1898, there were several large villages nearby, such as Chikanga, Manyarara, and Mandiambira. Unfortunately, those villages were affected by the Land Apportionment Act (1931) when most of the area surrounding Old Mutare Mission was declared European area. As all the Africans were moved to other areas, that was the end of the villages, and the churches that had mushroomed in those villages. The Christians who were scattered to other places became witnesses and leaders of the church in their new homes.

However, in 1903, before those villagers surrounding Old Mutare were banished, there were still few missionaries at the Mission. It is reported that the African preachers had taken the initiative to go out to those surrounding villages and conduct services.[141] That initiative by the African preachers was what Bishop Hartzell envisioned and hoped for. By 1909, churches and schools had been established in all the villages that surrounded Old Mutare Mission. For instance, Chikanga School, which had fifty students, and Maenzanise School were both under Solomon Joni. Manyarara School had 118 students with two pastor-teachers—Sanders Azwi and Isaiah (whose surname is not given). Mandiambira School had fifty students, with Obadiah Gapaza as the pastor-teacher.[142]

It was at Manyarara Methodist Church that Lydia Chimonyo experienced deep spiritual awakening. The site of the Manyarara Church is marked by one tall gum tree that still stands to this day, about six kilometres on the Old Mutare–Nyanga Road, before one reaches Manicabridge over the Odzani River. Briefly, the story is that Mbuya Chimonyo had gone to Manyarara to cultivate tsenza (a tropical tuberous plant), and then decided to attend an afternoon at a worship service in Manyarara Church. It was there that she found the Lord who appeared to her in the power of the Holy Spirit.[143]

In addition to the villages, Old Mutare Mission was also surrounded by about eleven mines. Some African preachers from the Mission preached in those mines and many people "professed conversion or the purpose to become Christians."[144] A number of those converts indicated the desire to go to the mission for training. The report says that practically every African village within thirty miles of Old Mutare Mission had been reached by the gospel by 1907,[145] and primarily through the initiative of the African preachers.

Mutasa Area

In 1903, Dr. Samuel Gurney visited *Guta ra*Mutasa (the official residential village of the chief), where he spent six weeks "studying the manners of the people, their religion, their attitude to the whites, etc."[146] After his visit, Dr. Gurney strongly recommended that the Methodist Episcopal Church begin work at Mutasa's *Guta* immediately.[147] Eddy Greeley's 1903 appointment sent him to the village *Guta ra*Mutasa. At the 1905 conference, he reported:

> In April 1904 I went to *kuGuta ra*Mutasa to begin work in that largest native town in Manikaland. The king received me cordially, and gave me a hut near his own. At last I thought, the Lord has put me where I so much longed to be ever since I came to Africa. I hoped my stay would be permanent. Jesus was my song by night and my prayer by day. I almost forgot the filthy little hut I lived in and the meager equipment I had for winning souls.[148]

Greeley stayed in the *Guta ra*Mutasa for some months sowing the seed of the gospel, which he hoped some day would ripen and converts would be made. In those days, Africans in villages often gathered together after supper for storytelling, sharing proverbs, and many other entertaining things. As people came to Greeley's hut, with many others sitting outside the house, he used that opportunity to teach them

Christian songs in the vernacular. He was involved in the healing ministry as well—curing ulcers, burns, cuts, and many other ailments. He believed he gave about six hundred treatments in all during his stay at *kuGuta*, and gives credit to Dr. Gurney who had carefully given him medical instruction.

From *Guta ra*Mutasa, Greeley visited Gonde, also known as Mundenda, a village where people had asked for a teacher to come and live in their midst.[149] Since it was difficult to find teachers to send to Mundenda at that time, a young man whose name is not given but who was teaching at Old Mutare, was supplying Mundenda voluntarily every weekend. By 1910, Mundenda had been opened and the native helper appointed there was Timothy (no surname is given). However, by 1909, evangelistic work in Mutasa area had led to the establishment of thirteen local churches that were supplied by seventeen native helpers and six Bible women.[150] The success of that evangelistic thrust in the Mutasa Circuit led to the purchase of land for the circuit headquarters, Nyakatsapa Mission.[151] Some of the native helpers who served in the developing circuit and had effectively taken the gospel to their own people included Isaac Chimbadzwa at Dowa, Peter Jamakanga at *kuGuta*, Nsingo at Katerera, John Mukahanana at Muredzwa, Jonah Kusekwa at Mapara, Lester Kachisi at Vumbunu, and Philip Useni at Sherukuru.[152]

There is a unique story about Chief Chakanyuka Mutasa, who participated in introducing the Methodist Episcopal Church to his chieftess, Sherukuru. Sherukuru United Methodist Church derives its name from the title the chieftess of the area holds to this day. The chieftess is a *muzvare*, meaning she is either a daughter or sister of Chief Mutasa. Sherukuru resided at Mapfekera, about ten kilometres north of Sherukuru United Methodist Church. A report presented to the 1908 mission conference had this to say about the chieftess:

> This Chieftess is the sister of the former King and is a superior native woman. She is head of part of the Inyanga District. At the Natives' request we opened work among them and it promises large. Congregation number 600 and over 72 are in school, 140 in Sunday school and a class of 40 will shortly be received on probation. The workers' house is complete and church is supported by the Switzerland Conference.[153]

In 1907, Chakanyuka, the reigning Mutasa, went to Sherukuru with some of his counselors and some African evangelists, including Samuel Matimba, who was then based at Mutasa's royal court. There was no missionary present. Chief Mutasa introduced the Methodist Episcopal Church to the Chieftess Sherukuru, who in turn did the same to the headman of the village, Kambanga, known as Kurewa, my own uncle. My mother, who was a young girl at that time, recalled a song that the evangelist Samuel Matimba taught them that day. The song is as follows:

Pindukayi madzimambo
Pindukai madzishe
Jesu watipindukayi
Muchidakuendawo kudenga
Mwari wati pindukayi

Repent chiefs
Repent sub-chiefs
Jesus says repent
If you want to go to heaven
God says you must repent.

Makoni Area

Earlier, we noted John Springer's trip to Gandanzara accompanied by ten students and helpers who were training to be teachers and evangelists, and his claim to be the first missionary to visit Gandanzara in 1905. At that first encounter, the sub-chief Gandanzara requested that Springer send a teacher.[154] Following the visit by Springer in January 1907, James Ferris and Shirley Coffin visited the sub-chief, Gandanzara, with the view of opening evangelistic and education work of the Methodist Episcopal Church among his people. Gandanzara, who initiated the idea, accompanied the two missionaries to Rusape to see the native commissioner concerning his request. Permission having been granted, Daniel Caplen and his wife, Mufambiswa, were appointed to begin work at Gandanzara immediately.[155] Both Caplen and Mufambiswa came from Nyassaland, although Mufambiswa had come out of a bitter experience. Some Mashona people who were returning from the northern journey stole her, and she was sold to some people in Southern Rhodesia. After some years, she ran away from her purchasers and went to Old Mutare Mission in June 1905. She was said to have been an unusually bright student, and there was married to Daniel Caplen, a well-known native-helper in the Methodist Episcopal Church.[156]

Later, Shirley Coffin shared a story about Gandanzara that the native commission of Rusape had shared with the missionaries. He said that prior to opening evangelistic and educational work at Gandanzara, the place had proved to be the worst village in his district. After the coming of the church, Gandanzara had become a Christian village. That says something about the transforming power of the Christian gospel.

By the 1908 mission conference, which was held at the end of 1907, both Svikiro and Mukahanana Methodist Episcopal churches had come into existence.[157] Ndingi and Zuze Methodist Episcopal churches also became part of the Gandanzara Circuit, but we do not have information on how and who started work in those places. However, by 1909 we learn from the journals that Stephen Mari "continues to do strong work" at Swikiro.[158] It seemed it was from Swikiro that Ndingi Methodist Episcopal Church was opened possibly by Stephen Mari. Mukahanana Methodist Episcopal Church was reported to be doing well by 1909 under the ministry of Samuel Matimba and his wife, Maringisenyi, who had just been married early in the year.

Methodist Episcopal missionaries found another African preacher already preaching the gospel independent of missionaries. Nehemiah Machakaire, who had been converted to Christianity by the former British Methodist Church while working in Salisbury, went back to his home, Muziti, in Makoni area, and started preaching to the people about his new faith. Many people were converted and Machakaire built a church big enough to accommodate between six hundred and seven hundred people. When Eddy Greeley visited Muziti, presumably in 1907 or 1908, he found a church already existed there. Machakaire accepted the invitation to join the Methodist Episcopal Church, and was subsequently appointed to take charge of the Muziti congregation.

Chapter 6

Evangelization of Murehwa and Its Frontier

As the Rhodesian government had treated Murehwa and Muto as one district, so the Methodist Episcopal Church treated Murehwa-Mutoko as a circuit, which was dominated by the leadership of Dr. Samuel Gurney, the missionary medical doctor.

Murehwa Mission

The first Methodist missionary to visit Murehwa area was John Springer. Soon after the adjournment of conference in June 1905, Springer, in the company of ten students and helpers who were training to become teachers and evangelists, visited Gandanzara, after which he proceeded northward to Murehwa where he found one of the largest villages in that part of Mashonaland.[159] In October of the same year, Springer went back to Murehwa and at that time Shirley Coffin accompanied him. It is quite possible that they were accompanied by some students or helpers again, although he does not say that specifically. The Murehwa people had had contact with traders and government officials for some time. However, there was no missionary work in the area. In April 1906, Springer, accompanied by his wife, made another trip to Murehwa and determined that a mission station should be established in the area. He discovered that the people in Murehwa were afraid, "lest a mission in their midst should curtail their liberty."[160]

In June 1908, E. L. Sechrist, an industrial teacher at Old Mutare went up to Murehwa, and upon his arrival found the people were not keen to see him. It took him three days before he saw Chief Mangwende, but when he finally met the chief he was graciously welcomed by him.

The chief allowed Sechrist and his students to visit and preach in every village of his people, but he would not allow them to put up a building in his area. Sechrist spent three months in the area and the missionary medical doctor Dr. Samuel Gurney spent some days with Sechrist in Mangwende's village. While Sechrist spent most of his time talking to the elderly people of the village, his students spoke to the young people. In a short time "phrases of gospel songs were to be heard here and there all over the village."[161]

One of Sechrist's concerns was the need for agricultural training in Murehwa. He observed that trees had been cut down leaving the land almost bare, the soil had been cultivated until it yielded no more, and the fields or gardens were so far away that people went there early in the morning and returned home in the evening. Therefore, the issue on his mind was:

> How can this country ever become fertile and fruitful until the people build permanent homes and till the soil properly instead of devastating tract after tract, denuding the whole country of vegetation and leaving it barren and desolate for years?[162]

After Sechrist returned to Old Mutare Mission, the task of opening Methodist Episcopal missionary work in the Murehwa area as well as in Mutoko became the responsibility of Dr. Gurney. Both Africans and white farmers in the area, in spite of the chief's resistance to establishing mission stations in his area, appreciated Dr. Gurney's work as a medical doctor. In fact, the Methodist Episcopal Church had deliberately sent Dr. Gurney in the Murehwa area "to see if the ministry of physical healing might not open the way to the hearts of the people and thus prepare them for the reception of the Gospel."[163] In spite of all that Dr. Gurney did among the people of Murehwa, and government efforts to overcome the fears of the chief, the chief insisted, "My heart does not want a mission in my country."[164] Both the Roman Catholic and the Anglican Churches also had earlier been denied entry into the area.

The government had a standing policy that missions should not be forced upon the people and therefore the consent of the chief had to be obtained before applying to the government for a site and official documentation. As much as the people seemed ready to welcome the Methodist Episcopal Church, the chief would not change his position. The native commissioner at Murehwa referred the matter to the native department of government in Salisbury. The reply came from the administrator that authority be given to the native department (in that special case) to grant mission sites even though the chief refused his consent. Dr. Gurney reported to the mission conference:

> And so the whole country is before us, and we are now at liberty to "go up and possess it." The responsibility for evangelising and saving the people of those two districts is upon us, and it seems as though God means that we shall do it, for His providence has closed the doors to all others and opened them widely for us. A great opportunity has been given us in that part of the country. May God help us to meet it wisely and faithfully.[165]

The missionaries who had frequented Murehwa area were interested in opening Methodist work in three places: Kanyasa village, Murehwa centre, and Murehwa location.

First, there was an attempt to establish a mission near Kanyasa village. It was Gurney's assessment that the people in that area were more eager for medicine than for teaching and preaching. However, by 1911 a school had been established, and the African teacher and preacher carried out an itinerant preaching programme to the surrounding villages. More and more people began to appreciate the work of the church in the area. At the same time, there was still opposition. Someone burned the teacher's house while he was away, and the culprit subsequently was arrested and jailed. The absence of a missionary caring for the sick in the villages and homes prevented that sort of work from being done. The Kanyasa mission never got into a position to operate as a mission station, although educational and evangelistic work continued in the surrounding villages.

Second, there were successful efforts to establish Murehwa Mission. Murehwa Mission has developed into a leading mission in the country. Unlike Mutambara, which started from nothing, the original site of Murehwa Mission "was formerly occupied as a trading station."[166] The place belonged to a trader, but upon his death, ownership of the site and building reverted to the government. The property consisted of a store, a four-room dwelling house, and several smaller houses, all of them built of poles and daagar. Like at Old Mutare Mission, in 1909:

> Through the kindness of the Government officials this site with all the buildings upon it was obtained for us at a cost of only the usual price of a lease for a mission site—one Pound.[167]

The mission station officially opened in the same year. Murehwa Mission had several advantages. Because of its proximity to the police camp, several white people in the police force, farmers, and those searching for gold often came to the mission station for medical treatment. Dr. Gurney had been appointed deputy District Surgeon by the government, which was willing to provide transport facilities, including cash compensation.[168] From Murehwa Mission, Dr. Gurney and his African helper went out on evangelistic tours in the villages to share the gospel. He also noted the white farmers and settlers working in government offices, including those who roamed over the district in search of gold, came to the mission centre for treatment. After such persons had spent a few days or weeks at the mission station, Dr.

Gurney reported, they left having dismissed the word *n*—— from their vocabulary, and with improved views as to what the church of God was doing in this country for both white and black. The gospel has power to change people, and indeed it works like yeast in a dough or gives better taste to things as does salt in food. It is quite possible that Dr. Gurney's African helper was Job Tamutsa (Job Tsiga), who was appointed to work at Murehwa in 1911 and was known to have worked with the medical doctor until the doctor's death. Job Tsiga became popularly known in the Zimbabwe Annual Conference as Sekuru (uncle) Tsiga, and died in 1975.

Third, in the report to the 1910 Mission Conference, Dr. Gurney talked about the possibility of opening a third mission station in the Murehwa area, at Murehwa location, about 22.5 kilometres from Murehwa Mission. It was a large village with about one thousand huts and an estimated population of about 3,500 people, probably the largest village in the country. Like the rest of the Murehwa area, there was no mission work there. The way for missionary work had been opened by one event that Dr. Gurney reported:

> The chief of that section—who stood by and witnessed an important surgical operation that saved the life of his child—has given his consent for our opening a mission in his kraal. We have made formal application to the government for a mission site there; the native commissioner has sent his recommendation that it be granted, and he has reported to us that the government is ready to grant it as soon as we are ready for it. But we are not ready for we have no one to send there. The fields are ripe for the harvest, but there are no reapers.[169]

The first bishop's appointees to Murehwa were Dr. Samuel Gurney and one unnamed African helper in 1909. The number was increased to four in 1910 as Edward McLean, John Potter, and James Apiri were added. Potter worked in the Murehwa Location while Apiri was in Kanyasa area. Although the Kanyasa mission did not get off the ground, there was still work to be done in the surrounding villages.

Mutoko Mission

In his report of 1910, Dr. Gurney spoke emphatically of opening another mission station at Mutoko, about sixty-five kilometres north of Murehwa. Mutoko area had a large population and the native commission was friendly and looked favourably on the work of the Methodist Episcopal Church. Dr. Gurney perceived the idea of opening a mission at Mutoko as a way to move on from there toward Nyanga. He saw the work in Mutoko as a final link that would connect Methodist work in Mutasa area. Early in 1911, the government gave the old police camp, which contained several good brick buildings to the Methodist Episcopal Church to start missionary work in the area. By 1912 the appointments in the Murehwa-Mutoko Circuit included Dr. Gurney as head of Murehwa Mission, with medical work as his special responsibility; Solomon Gebeto was appointed to Kanyasa, Aramu Mukumbo at Marimesi, Jeremiah Nyakuengama at Murehwa location, and James Apiri at Mutoko.

In 1915, the bishop appointed Isaiah Kashayanyama (Isaiah Munjoma) to Mutoko, and by 1917 Eddy Greeley became the first resident missionary at Mutoko. The bishop also appointed Paul Malianga and Joseph Nyamurowa as pastor-teachers to the new mission.[170]

Nyadiri Mission

Despite the fact that Nyadiri Mission was established after 1921, the limit of the scope of this book, we include it here because the planning of Nyadiri Mission was integral to the Murehwa-Mutoko programme by Dr. Gurney. Nyadiri Mission is about forty kilometres north of Murehwa, and the farm on which the mission is situated was acquired in August 1922.[171] Thomas O'Farrell, then the superintendent of the Murehwa

District, presented the rationale for buying what became known as the Nyadiri Mission farm:

> The location is ideal if we consider Murehwa and Mutoko government Districts as a unit of work and build up a medical and an educational institution there strong enough to minister to the total area. We have there a very large and valuable field. Within the bounds of this District is a population of 55,000 people still available for us, a territory and population sufficient to justify the entire work that any Missionary Society is now doing in Rhodesia.[172]

The first bishop's appointees to Nyadiri Mission were Dr. Sumuel Gurney and L. E. Tull in 1923. The emphasis of the Nyadiri Mission from the beginning was medical work. Consequently, a dispensary building was built immediately in 1923. Fortunately for the mission, early in the year of 1924, three missionaries arrived at Nyadiri: Miss Quinton, Miss Clark, and Miss Ramsey. But sadly, the person behind establishing the medical institution at Nyadiri Mission, Dr. Gurney, died in Harare on 3 August 1924.[173] This was a big blow to the young conference, and especially to the people who had worked so closely with the medical doctor.

A school for girls was started at Nyadiri in 1925; one for boys was started later. Like other mission stations, a large population surrounded Nyadiri, and it therefore became an influential mission station from which evangelistic, educational, and especially medical work was launched to the surrounding villages. Today, Nyadiri stands majestically as the centre for medical work in terms of the number of patient beds and also in the training of nurses.

PART THREE

SEARCHING FOR IDENTITY

In this part of the book, we find that both the church and African pastor-teachers are searching for a new identity. With the coming of the 1918 Revival, the church in Southern Rhodesia discovered new and cultural expressions of the Christian faith. The *Vabvuwi* (Men's Organization) group explored new ways of presenting the gospel through singing, which developed to the use of African instruments such as the drum, *hosho* (calabash), and others. Similarly, the native helper image blossomed to that of an elder in the Methodist Episcopal Church, a great achievement both for the church and the individual elders. All of a sudden the African people began to realize they were the church of Christ in Africa and not just a mission field of the churches from overseas.

Chapters 7, 8, and 9 show how the image of both the Methodist Episcopal Church in Southern Rhodesia and its African preachers are transformed in history by the power of the gospel that the church propagated.

Chapter 7

The African Pastor-Teacher

An informal discussion on how to recognize the native workers or native helpers took place at the first session of the East Central Africa Mission Conference of the Methodist Episcopal Church held in Mutare. The unanimous opinion was that the powers to be conferred on native pastors and workers had to be done wisely, with great care, and that conservatism was to be exercised.[174] These native workers were, and had to be, regarded as helpers. Subsequently, anything cultural and social, such as African marriage customs and other cultural practices, were questioned by the missionaries.[175] When Africans came to live at mission stations either as employees or students they were literally stripped of their cultural and social practices. No wonder the discussion on Native Marriage Laws at the first session of the mission conference immediately led to a resolve to refuse full "membership in the Church to any native having more than one wife."[176]

Interestingly and encouragingly, the number of Methodist native helpers who served as preachers and interpreters both in the Portuguese East Africa and Southern Rhodesia districts, increased year after year. Following the creation of the two mission conferences, namely the Portuguese East Africa Mission Conference and the Rhodesia Mission Conference at the eleventh session of the East Central Africa Mission Conference,[177] the native helpers were listed in the official journals of the Rhodesia Mission Conference for the first time as "native pastor-teachers," beginning with the 1917 session of the Rhodesia Mission Conference.[178] By 1917, the native pastor had become a strong force of about twenty-eight African preachers of the Methodist

Episcopal Church deployed in mission stations, urban centres, and church-schools in the villages. It is important that the reader become acquainted with the names of the people who were first recognized as pastor-teachers in the history of Methodism in Zimbabwe:

Andrew Fari Mahlukira
Andrew Watap Murahwa
Anderson Mwachande Kachisi
Andrew Mbengo Mahechani
Alpheus Selu Nyatanga
Benjamin Jongwe Karimupfumbi
Benjamin Rimayi Katsidzira
Benjamin Misi Kawadza
Clifford Edward Faku
David Mazotwa Mandisodza
Daniel Gatawa Chitenderu
Enoch Pungura Munjoma
Furnes Chatepa
Gilbert Ringayi Rakabopa
Isaac Nhamo Kajau
Isaiah Shati Darikwa
Isaiah Matawa Munjoma
Isaiah Mujeya Musamaba
Isaiah Mupepwa Thichiwanhunyi
James Vilika
James Manyope Chukuse
Job Tamutsa Tsiga
Job Tirase Gondora
John Muguri Mugwambi
Johnson Mukaronda Maramba
Johnson Marambachinyi Sachiti
Jonah Goto Chiyeza
Joseph Chimuzabwe Nyamurowa
Joseph Murauro
Jonah Gurungo Chikwariro
Jason Chambokoni Chikosi
Moses Paradzayi Muparutsa
Moses Hamudi Chisamba
Nathan Mahowa Gwishiri
Nathan Mandipemhesa Gwizo
Nathaniel Jim Jijita
Gezana Sadomba
Obadiah Gapaza Chimonyo
Obadiah Dubuhlingwi Mawaro
Paul Chivaku Chiwanga
Peter Dzayiko Mafunde
Philip Zikiti Chiyeza
Benton Clephas John Vilika
Samuel Sekayi Chiyeza
Simeon Zinarenyi Machiri
Solomon Gebetu Mapara
Thomas Muchenje Marange
Thomas Muziti[179]

Status of the Pastor-Teacher

The pastor-teacher was different from a native helper, and in some cases one might have begun his career as native helper and rose to the position of a pastor-teacher. While the term *native helper* was inclusive, the term *pastor-teacher* was more specific. *Pastor-teacher* referred to a church leader in the community who performed his work as a teacher during the weekdays, as well as assuming pastoral duties during the seven days of the week. Since the educational institutions that flourished throughout the land toward the end of the nineteenth century and the beginning of the twentieth century were established by the churches, that led toward the development of African leadership in and of the church. In other words, the pastor-teachers became recognized leaders in the communities where the church sent them. Consequently, in those early days pastor-teachers ranked among the highly educated African people and as leaders with a regular income. Their children were among those who received higher education in the country, with others going to South Africa. Their children were among those who became prominent teachers in the mission schools, interpreters in the law courts, medical doctors, and many other professions. The community in general acknowledged the pastor-teachers families as better than those in a given community. Their families became envied by others.

It needs to be pointed out, however, that neither the term *native helper* nor *pastor-teacher* was an order of the ministry of the Methodist Episcopal Church. Those were simply titles that were used conveniently by the church to designate its African leadership. What is important about the designations of *native helper* and *pastor-teacher* is that as part of the history and development of the church they also served as the foundation of understanding and appreciating the ministry of the Methodist Episcopal Church in Southern Rhodesia. Every pastor-teacher in the Methodist Episcopal Church had to meet some required standards. In

1919, Old Mutare Mission established the Training School, composed of three departments: Theological, Literary and Normal, and Industrial. In the department of theological education, the students studied the following courses: the Bible, homiletics, church history, and studies in Christian doctrine. In the Literary and Normal department, the emphasis was to upgrade the training of African teachers, once referred to as native teachers. The church in the United States actually sent trained missionaries from America for that purpose. In the Industrial department, only one branch of industry—wood and brickwork—was taught. Later, agriculture also was taught in the same department. The emphasis of the church then was to produce qualified African leaders for both the church and society. The qualification expected of every graduate from the three departments at Old Mutare Mission "was two-fold: educational and spiritual."[180] The educational qualifications were to "include an ability to teach the people how to make better native gardens and how to erect a simple house of brick and to make simple furniture."[181] In the Report of the Committee on Evangelism of 1919, the philosophy of education for those studying to become pastor-teachers was clearly stated:

> Those who are to be teachers as well as preachers should have normal training and the best literary training our Central School can give them. They should have simple lessons in sermonising and in Christian doctrine and such studies as are taught in the Theological Department of the Central Training School . . . Spiritually no pastor-teacher or evangelist should be sent out, no matter what educational qualifications he may possess, without giving evidence of a definite conversion. He should have upon his heart a burden for the salvation of the people and live a life of prayer.[182]

Those were the standards expected of all pastor-teachers, and the mission conference had to pass judgment on the character of each one of them at each session annually before appointment to their respective places by the bishop.

One notable factor that our generation of pastors may need to learn from the pioneer pastor-teachers is that at the time of their retirement, a good number of them were able to purchase land in areas that had been demarcated as African Purchase Areas, places such as in Zimunya area, Musengezi area, or Tsonzo area. In other words, knowing the church did not have a sustaining scheme of pension, they were able prepare for their retirement.

A Sense of Vocation

The pastor-teacher performed his work not merely as a duty, but also ideally as a vocation—a calling from God. He taught classes from Monday through Friday and preached on Sunday. He prepared candidates for baptism, confirmation, and for receiving Holy Communion. He traveled to all the churches that were under his charge to bury the dead. He was indeed the pastor of his flock. Often he traveled long distances to preach the gospel and to plant new churches, often becoming responsible for up to ten churches. Both Joseph Nyamurowa and James Chikuse narrate interesting experiences about their work. The following statement was part of Joseph Nyamurowa's report to the 1917 session of the Rhodesia Mission Conference of the Methodist Episcopal Church.

> I commenced work at Mutoko on February 1, 1917 and the work in school is now running nicely. I have 46 scholars marked in the register. The regular attendance who come most every day is about 30–35. My wife has one class for women. On Sunday mornings I go out in the kraals with some helpers to preach about the true God, yet the people

> do not seem to believe in him as their Saviour because many of these are full of heathenism. In these different villages we preach to are many kraals and people, but I do not know how many of these huts are dotted all over the land, and that means that both people are scattered away to their gardens to watch the baboons, and some of them have made their homes at their gardens on account of the horrible baboons [he then names 13 villages where he goes to preach on foot, with the nearest 1 hour away, and farthest 2.5 hours away,]. . . But there are many more kraals, which are unreached, and I am earnest expecting to reach them as soon as I can.[183]

James Chikuse sounds original and I credit him as a contextual theologian. In his narration he uses the term *boys* the way colonialists and some missionaries of his time used to refer to African men. Below is what he shared at the session of 1917 of the Rhodesia Mission Conference of the Methodist Episcopal Church.

> When I was at Marara I call boys [colonialists and missionaries called every man a "boy" regardless of his age] together to have meeting all together. I said to them, what is mean to say church, they say to say church is to say teacher. I said No, to say church is you boys you connect yourselves together in Christianity, and I show them two poles which stand between the church to hold up the roof, and I say, if this two poles said, I am tired we must go to somewhere, can this roof stand? They said No, they will go down. I said what will that do? They said that will break the walls poles and all things and I said, Yes you know that boys that will break all things. You are the poles of the church, if you get out, you will kill your wife

> and children and mother and father. Stand still like these poles and I said God said to Moses one night, he said to him, let Joshua go with Israel people tomorrow to frighten the Amalekites, you Aaron and Hur on the hill lift up the rod. Moses, did what God told him. At noontime Moses got his hands tired, he went to put his hands down, and Aaron came to the right hand and Hur to the left hand to support Moses to save his people from dying. Boys do like these two poles. Stand still like Aaron and Hur.[184]

A Theological Reflection

As we reflect upon the concept of a pastor-teacher, we are often tempted to say that this could have been an appropriate model of pastoral ministry for the churches in Africa. There are two elements that are imbedded in that idea, namely a holistic approach to life and a holistic philosophy about theological education.

First, a holistic approach to life: lest we forget, Old Mutare Mission was established as an industrial mission for the African people. The message of the early missionaries of the Methodist Episcopal Church in Zimbabwe was indeed holistic in emphasis. Similarly, the requests that came from many chiefs to the missionaries were for both a teacher and an evangelist as they saw both teaching and evangelism going hand in hand. In his report to the 1905 mission conference, John Springer said:

> In the education of the African, as with all races, we believe that no principle is more important to inculcate than that industry comes first in a good life, and that one should earn his food and the right to schooling before receiving them.[185]

Following that principle, it is not surprising that some of the African leaders who became known later as native helpers or pastor-teachers started their leadership life as garden "boys" or domestic "boys" either in missionaries homes or in a colonial settler's home. While they performed their duties as garden or domestic boys, they learned to respect work as well. Bishop Taylor believed that missionaries should be self-supporting. This idea could have been extended to African pastors as well, to some extent. The idea, in spite of its limitations, was a good one. It needs to continue to be explored, and instilled in our people, especially our African pastors.

There seems to be a misconception in some people, including pastors, that the work of a pastor is simply praying, preaching, reading, and pastoral visitation alone, ruling out spending some time in a garden, planting trees around the parsonage yard, and other manual jobs. There could be some people who are running away from the world of work into the ministry of the church because there they are opposed to manual work. Trusting in the guidance of God should not be allowed to become a spiritual illusion. Thus, some of the time spent in prayer, even pastoral visitation, could be utilized doing manual work around the house to support and supply the needs of the family. The fact that Jesus said to the tempter, "Man does not live on bread alone" (Matt. 4:4) shows bread plays a significant, nutritious role in life. But often that food comes to the table through hard work, at times through the hard work of our hands. Paul says, "Make it your ambition to lead a quiet life, to mind your own business and to work with your hands" (1 Thess. 4:11). He also says, "If a man will not work, he shall not eat" (2 Thess. 3:10).

The support that pastors receive today from parishioners is good, but the African pastor-teachers of almost a hundred years ago were not shy to learn to support themselves by doing some gardening, repairs around the house, and other manual work.

That concept of a holistic philosophy to life caught fire, not only among the pastor-teachers, but also with the laity. In The United Methodist Church, the name Abraham Kawadza will long be remembered. Abraham became a leading lay evangelist before the 1920s, partly because of his commitment to the Christian faith, which removed fear and superstition and made him a successful farmer. He was the first African to use a plough in the Odzani area. A retired pastor-teacher, Mutambanengwe became a successful farmer by overcoming the superstition about a place known as Dambakurimwa (a place that refused to be cultivated). People had believed that if anyone cut down any of its trees, the following morning those trees would be found restored. By felling the trees he found one of the most fertile soils for cultivation, and in that way became a successful layperson and preacher in the Methodist Church.

By 1925, Methodist Episcopal Church families had taken the lead in their communities, improving agriculture through the use of the plough, and George Roberts pointed out how the plough in the hands of the Christian people revolutionized places such as Gandanzara, Mukahanana, Buwu, and others.[186] Hence, in those days the Methodists talked about the "gospel of the plough." Speaking about the gospel of the plough, George Roberts had this to say:

> A farmer storekeeper in that section has a sale of five or six steel ploughs per week. The sale of agricultural products from that section of our work is most inspiring. These people are no longer a poverty-stricken people. Go over, if you will, to a certain part of the Inyanga District, and you will find hundreds of potato gardens which are bringing much money to the Christian and also slightly trained people. I have seen 130 baskets of potatoes going into Umtali on a single market day from Buwu and the surrounding stations. The people have Paul Chigawa and Daniel Chitenderu [pastor-teachers] to thank for placing this weapon against poverty in their hands.[187]

The message of early Methodists in Southern Rhodesia was holistic, for salvation meant saving the whole person—meeting the need of many Africans who had all along sought to worship God in spirit and truth. That gospel in its holistic nature challenged people to love God with their heart, their soul, their mind, and their strength.

Second, there was a holistic philosophy about theological education: one of the issues that the church in Africa may want to think about seriously is the concept of the pastor-teacher as an appropriate model for the pastoral ministry today. It is for that reason that I congratulate the early fathers of the Methodist Episcopal Church in Southern Rhodesia for holding a holistic philosophy about theological education as they established the church in this country. A missionary who wrote about India in the 1950s said, "A full-time, salaried minister is considered alien to the religious cultures of some sections of Asia and Africa."[188]

There could be some truth in the above quotation. In the African traditional communities no religious leader was ever considered as a full-time religious leader. The chief, who poses as the highest religious and priestly authority of his people, would never think of himself as a religious leader exclusively. As a matter of fact, in Zimbabwe's past, the chief would have his own *zunde ramambo*—a field exclusively for the chief, without his wives involvement. His subjects cultivated the field, and the chief used the harvests to help the needy, again, without making a burden on his wives. Yet he was a religious leader. As much as the chief had other traditional religious leaders, such as *n'anga yamambo*—a traditional healer of the chief and his family, or one *munayisi wemvura*—the rainmaker, such traditional religious leaders were not full-time, and neither did they rely on the people or on the chief for their livelihood. They performed their duties as they were needed. Indeed, there is a sense in which the pastor-teacher model of Christian ministry in Africa was in line with the African model of traditional religious leadership.

If The United Methodist Church had continued with the model of pastor-teachers, the model would have been justified on the following grounds:

(a) The church would have developed the training of pastors on the model of a pastor-carpenter. Was Jesus not known first as a carpenter? "Isn't this the carpenter?" (Mark 6:3) the people of Nazareth asked when they heard Jesus teaching in the synagogue on the Sabbath. Indeed, during the week they had known him as a carpenter. It is possible that Jesus might have gone up and down the roads of Nazareth selling furniture to the citizens of that town. That was how the dwellers of Nazareth first came to know Jesus. But he had also become a pastor-carpenter who "taught them as one who had authority" (Mark 1:22).

(b) The church could have developed the training of pastors on the model of pastor-agriculturalists. It must have been for that reason, in some regions of India, the church resorted to the training of rural pastors, whose training embraces both rich theological scholarship and an emphasis in the specifics of rural life.[189] In India, a rural pastor who has one or more of the following, "a garden, a flock of improved fowls, some fruit trees, a cow or a goat, some bees, a few rabbits,"[190] provides a helpful demonstration to his members of the fullness of life that Jesus talks about in John 10:10. He or she quickly receives acceptance by the people—both those in and outside the church.

(c) The church also would have developed the training of our pastors on the model of pastor-businessman or businesswoman. Aquila and his wife, Priscilla, were business people and yet great evangelists who worked quietly in Corinth. They were tentmakers, and it was for that reason Paul was attracted to them (Acts 18:3). Likewise, Paul, also a tentmaker, wrote to the Thessalonians, "Surely you remember, brothers, our toil and hardship; we worked night and day in order not to be a burden to anyone while we preached the gospel of God to you" (1 Thess. 2:9). Although tentmaker could mean many other things, "Recent scholars have realised that Paul literally means that he had been working full time and had used his place of business as a point of contact with people to proclaim the gospel."[191] Paul and his two companions, Silas and Timothy, arrived in Thessalonica and probably rented a

Roman *insula*—a two- or three-story apartment. While they used the upper rooms as living quarters, the ground floor was a place to operate their leather business. While their business gave them an income to take care of their expenses, the main purpose for the business on the ground floor was to make contact with people—creating an opportunity to share or communicate the gospel of Jesus Christ. Paul, Silas, and Timothy were indeed, tentmakers—pastor-businessmen.

(d) The church would have developed a training model of the pastor-health worker. Again, as Edward Ziegler says, it is not enough, when preventable death occurs, to say, "The Lord gave and the Lord has taken away" (Job 1:21). In relation to training pastors for village ministry, Ziegler sees the need for a pastor who understands and is able to support "the agencies concerned with the control of epidemics, the purification of water, improvement of home sanitation, family care, mosquito control, nutritional instruction,"[192] and many others. We could have easily followed the model of the early Methodist pastor-teachers, and today we would have pastor-health workers. Maybe that way we would have overcome the idea of a "full-time and salaried minister" with its disastrous results.

Chapter 8

Pastor-Teachers and the 1918 Revival

A dictionary definition of the word *revival* is "a bringing or coming back into use, attention, or being after a decline."[193] The biblical meaning of *revival* is generally agreed upon as to be renewed or flourish anew. "The image is that of a plant flourishing again after a time of drought."[194] It is in that spirit that Paul was overjoyed by the saints in Christ at Philippi, who had revived their thoughtful and caring concern for Paul, not necessarily for Paul's sake, but for their own sake. "I rejoice greatly in the Lord that at last you have renewed your concern for me," Paul writes in Philippians 4:10. One can only imagine that the renewal of faith in the life of the Philippian church became contagious enough to touch and fill Paul's heart with great joy. That was a revival, and what a revival is meant to be.

In Zimbabwe Episcopal Area, it appears *revival* and *evangelism* are understood to mean the same thing. Samuel Dzobo says:

> Revivals are main events on a United Methodist congregation's calendar. Each local church or charge will have a minimum of four revival meetings as organized by the youth, women, men and the evangelism committee for the local church. The district will also have a minimum of four revival meetings. The conference usually has three revival meetings, but the women's revival meetings or the conventions dominate because of the large numbers of people who attend.[195]

The history of revival meetings' success has meant that clergy and laity now define evangelism in connection with revivalism. That means the United Methodists in the Zimbabwean Annual Conferences, and most probably of all annual conferences of The United Methodist Church in Africa, tend to use the terms *revival* and *evangelism* interchangeably. Or they do their evangelism through what they call *revival meetings*.

Origin of the Revival

Some older members of the church and a number of preachers often make reference to the revival of 1918. My parents traced their conversion to the revival of 1918, and consequently always wanted me learn as much as I could about it. On a few occasions I have been asked to speak on the subject. It is still difficult to pinpoint exactly how the revival started. What seems clear in the official reports to the 1919 Rhodesia Mission conference is that the Holy Spirit had come upon the seventeen-year-old conference.

First, there was a Report of the Committee on Resolutions that acknowledged the revival as following:

> Since God has so graciously answered the prayers that have ascended to Him for Africa from the missionaries, the native Christians and the church at home, our hearts are filled with gratitude to him for the revival that visited our work beginning last June, and which reached almost every heart.[196]
>
> Second, a report of district superintendents, which stated the following:
>
> Just as it should be, the past year has been unquestionably our best year. Great new spiritual values have been realized. Every centre has been shaken with a fresh spiritual

> blast until heathen people have seen a great light and felt the presence of a new power.[197]
>
> Third, another report about the impact of the revival came from the Committee on the State of the Church, which stated: Last June there came upon our native teachers a baptism—a Pentecost. We are not impressed with gymnastics that some went through, but a large number of our men became flaming fires with a heavy burden for their people rolled upon them.[198]

The above-mentioned conference reports acknowledge and confirm that a great happening had taken place in the history and life of the Rhodesia Mission Conference that had been born in 1901—namely, a revival.

There are still members in The United Methodist Church today who attribute the origin of their faith journey, or even more so that of their parents, with the 1918 revival. The Holy Spirit event of 1918 stands out in the history of The United Methodist Church in Zimbabwe to this day as a modern-day Pentecost. It is said that it all began with the first camp meeting for pastor-teachers, commencing on 4 June 1918. Oral tradition about the event says that it began with an African school girl at Rusitu Mission, south of Mutare, which belongs to what is now the United Church of Christ. The little girl triggered the event with a testimony that she shared with others. The official journals of the Methodist Episcopal Church, however, start with James Hatch, a missionary of the United Church of Christ, who came to Old Mutare Mission with other Christians just at the time when the first camp meeting for the pastor-teachers of the Methodist Episcopal Church had been convened. In an afternoon service Hatch preached, telling people the wonderful things God had done among the people at Rusitu Mission, and the way the Holy Spirit had come upon them.

It is possible that Hatch could be the source of the story about the schoolgirl who triggered the revival at Rusitu through her testimony. Those who came with Hatch witnessed to the same events. Some of the missionaries at Old Mutare laughed at their visitors, calling them false prophets. However, late in the afternoon that same day, when Hatch was preaching again, the church is said to have been filled with various noises from people. There was little sleeping for some people that following night, for while some went to bed, others stayed in the church, and prayed incessantly throughout the night; singing and shouting went on. One of the reporters of the revival, Janson Machiwenyika, an African teacher at Old Mutare Mission, put it bluntly: "That day our Methodist Church was filled with the Holy Spirit and it became clear in our minds that Reverend Hatch had really said what he had perceived."[199]

Like at the original Pentecost, reporters of the 1918 revival experience found it difficult to describe exactly what happened other than people were filled with the Holy Spirit. We have noted Machiwenyika's testimony that "our Methodist Church was filled with the Holy Spirit"; we also have noted that the Conference Special Committee on the State of the Church reported the event as "a baptism—a Pentecost" on the African pastor-teachers. Indeed, even though some missionaries laughed about the revival happenings, the conference received the Report of Committee on Resolutions, which opened by stating:

> Since God has so graciously answered the prayers that have ascended to Him from the missionaries, the native Christians, and the church at home, our hearts are filled with gratitude to Him for the revival that visited our work beginning last June, and which reached almost every heart.[200]

While some missionaries wanted to associate the revival with the pastor-teachers, the church as whole was renewed.

Conference-wide Revival

After Hatch had preached and the following night when some people spent the night listening to preaching, praying, praising God, and testimonies, the camp meeting for the pastors was interrupted by divine intervention. Immediately, the pastor-teachers were sent to other mission stations, towns, and village churches to proclaim Jesus Christ in the power of the Holy Spirit, and to give testimony of what had happened at Old Mutare Mission. That led to the spreading of the revival to other mission stations and to all the out-stations of the Methodist Episcopal Church that were visited. Through the official journals of the church we can still experience the emotion of church leaders who shared their testimonies at the following mission conference session.

First was a testimony from Pearl Mullikin, a missionary stationed at Old Mutare whose responsibility was literary work and Bible. In giving her missionary report, Mullikin concluded by sharing a testimony of personal experience:

> I have been here for more than three years, but only within the last year have I been able to say, "Thy will be done" with reference to staying at Old Mutare. Since that night nearly a year ago I have been happy. I am willing to go or stay, whichever seems best to the Bishop. "He has brought me out more than a conqueror."[201]

Second, from Nyakatsapa Mission and Mutasa Circuit is a testimony from John Praisley. For over three years, the Mutasa Circuit had had no supervision; probably meaning it had no missionary who supervised it. John Praisley and his wife, who were due for furlough back home, spent three months in Cape Town waiting in vain—due to war conditions there were no ships available. As a result, they returned to the field, and were sent to Nyakatsapa Mission about early July, and just in time for the July quarterly meeting. Praisley is one of the few missionaries who not only spoke positively about the revival, but who also claimed to be the beneficiary of it. This is what he had to say about the quarterly meeting experience:

> From the very first meeting it was evident that that the Spirit of the Lord was at work, but not until the third day came direct manifestation of a real Pentecost. Such a scene my wife and I will never forget, and is best described in the second chapter of Acts, "And they were all filled with the Holy Ghost and began to speak with other tongues as the Spirit gave them utterance."[202]

The attendance at the October quarterly meeting was the largest they had ever had at that circuit, there being about five hundred present. Praisley points out between the quarterly meetings of July and October a number of evangelists or pastor-teachers had been at work, so much so that the whole circuit was in a fairly good condition for a gathering of that many people. In spite of the fact that the circuit had been without missionary supervision for almost three years, as Praisley visited all the out-stations, he found in each place what he described as "the fires of revival smoldering and burning."[203]

Third, from Mutambara, George Roberts reported that Mutambara Mission had received a great spiritual uplift as a result of the revival. Many people had been converted, confessed their sins and accepted Jesus Christ as their Saviour. And some had returned property they had stolen. Roberts goes on to report that the spiritual awakening had also visited the out-stations, such as Chatora and Mutsiyabako.[204]

Impact of the Revival

First, in reporting to the 1919 conference, we have already noted the expression of thanksgiving and gratitude to God by the Committee on Resolutions. The district superintendents shared a list of what they conceived to be the fruits of the revival:

(a) The spirit of evangelism moved many, especially the pastor-teachers, to go from village to village preaching and witnessing to the gospel.
(b) For the first time a great number of people were brought to a saving knowledge of the Son of God.
(c) New out-stations were opened at the rate of about one a month.
(d) Some closed stations were re-opened.
(e) Forty or more African young men volunteered for Christian service.
(f) Church, Sunday school, and day school attendance had gradually increased at most of the mission stations and out-stations.
(g) More land was acquired for the erection of several brick and iron buildings, in addition to about fifteen out-station churches that already existed.
(h) The financial income had increased to over a thousand pounds.[205]

Second, the revival had great impact upon the African pastor-teachers. No wonder the report of the Committee on the State of the Church reads, "Last June there came upon our native teachers a baptism—a Pentecost." The revival changed the African pastor-teachers; it gave them a new confidence, not only in what the gospel could do, but also in what God could do through them. They realized their potential as instruments of God. They had come to realize a new identity of themselves in God's hand. All of a sudden the concept of being considered as helpers began to vanish, as they realized they were in the forefront of sharing the gospel among their own people. If anything, they realized they were the ones who needed helpers in the Lord's harvest.

Third, the revival had an impact on some of the missionaries. We noted testimonies from Pearl Mullikin, John Praisley, and even three missionaries who constituted the Committee of Resolutions.

Fourth, the revival launched the conference paper *Umbowo hweUkristu*—the Christian Witness—in 1918.[206] It is not clear that the paper was launched as a direct result of the revival; nevertheless it was launched during the year when the revival flourished. Eddy Greeley was the first editor of the paper, and he indicated that the pastor-teachers and some of the church people always appreciated receiving and reading the paper.

Fifth, the revival impacted the life of the Methodist Episcopal Church by making it apparent that Sunday school work was one of the most fruitful factors of the church's evangelistic ministry during their time.[207] Sunday school provided as an opportunity for young men, women, and children to come together to learn more about the Christian faith, the Bible, and Christian family life. The church sought to train teachers for Sunday school and to provide teaching materials for their members. With the establishment of the printing press in 1918, the conference was able to produce Sunday school reading materials for its members throughout the conference, which is not the case today.

Sixth, the *Vabvuwi* Organisation of the Methodist Episcopal Church was a direct result of the 1918 revival.[208] Although we do not know exactly how the organisation began, we know that as the revival spread from place to place, a band of men or "volunteer band" as they were known in the conference, "organised themselves to continue that practice as a permanent way of doing evangelism." In those early days of the organisation, it was known by the name *marombe* (homeless people). In this case it meant people who had left their homes, families, and everything else for Christ. Some of the members of the organisation took the meaning of the term *marombe* too literally. For they thought it meant abandoning responsibility for their wives and families and adopting an asceticism that abandoned rules of cleanliness. Eventually the name *marombe* was dropped, and was replaced by *vabvuwi* (fishermen). As early as January 1921, the Old Mutare vabvuwi organisation sponsored David Mandisodza's trip to Harare in pursuit of Methodist Episcopal Church members who found employment there. That trip led to Mandisodza's appointment to Harare after his scouting trip in the same year.[209]

Finally, the revival had its miracles, too. There were manifestations of the glory of Christ that people believed to be the work of God. There is one miracle in particular almost every member of the Methodist Episcopal Church in Zimbabwe must have heard about in one way or another. The story is told that around June or July 1918, Nhenhu Muredzwa, a daughter of Ishe (Chieftess) Muredzwa of Zinyembe (a royal sister of Chief Mutasa), was about six years old when her hands and legs became deformed. The cause of the deformity was not known, despite all the consultation of diviners. Nhenhu spent her days lying down and had to be carried everywhere. As the revival spread in Chief Mutasa's area, African pastor-teachers John Cheke, David Mandisodza, Gezana Sadomba, and others who were at Old Mutare when the revival broke out, arrived in Zinyembe, Chieftess Murezwa's area, to preach the gospel. Naturally, everyone began to talk about the preachers in the area. Nhenhu, the disabled chieftess's daughter, wanted to see and hear the witness of the preachers for herself. Oral tradition says that after obtaining permission from her mother, the chieftess, Nhenhu invited the preachers to the house where she lived. The pastor-teachers and the other Christians present engaged themselves in singing and after a season of prayer, Gezana Sadomba got up and held Nhenhu from her armpits, with David Mandisodza laying his hands on her head. While everyone was in the spirit of prayer and great expectation, John Cheke repeated the Apostle's words, "In the name of Jesus Christ of Nazareth, walk" (Acts 3:6). As they lifted her, for the first time in a long time Nhenhu stood and walked. Nhenhu, Murezwa's daughter, was baptized and became known as Dorcas. She is said to have been member of the Methodist Episcopal Church until her death in July 1972.[210]

Chapter 9

The Making of *Mufundisi*

Finally, after twenty years the African pastor-teacher came to be accepted as one who had been called of God and as a capable leader. The first African pastor-teacher to be ordained deacon in the Rhodesia Mission Conference of the Methodist Episcopal Church by Bishop Eben Johnson was David Mandisodza at Old Mutare Mission on 19 June 1921.[211] That historic ordination was followed by another ordination of six pastor-teachers as deacons at Nyadiri Mission on 7 November 1926. Those new deacons were Isaiah Darikwa, Clifford Faku, Benjamin Katsidzira, Thomas Marange, Titus Marange, and Isaiah Munjoma.[212] Reginald Ngonyama and Gezana Sadomba were ordained deacons at Old Mutare Mission on 19 June 1927,[213] and Josiah Chimbadzwa, Zachariah Mukombiwa, and Joseph Nyamurowa were ordained deacons at Old Mutare Mission on 16 September 1928.[214]

However, the greatest milestone in the history of the development of African indigenous ministry in the Methodist Episcopal Church was when four African deacons—Clifford Faku, David Mandisodza, Thomas Marange, and Reginald Ngonyama—were ordained elders in 1929.[215] This meant that for the first time in its twenty-eight-year history in the country, the Methodist Episcopal Church had developed an African indigenous leadership that was capable of preaching the Word and administering the sacraments to its own people. And for the four newly ordained elders, it was not only an institutional achievement of their church, but also great personal achievement.

As the new order of African-ordained leadership emerged at the end of the 1920s in Zimbabwe, from time to time a number of questions must have come to mind for those new leaders. I say this because even to this day when United Methodism in Zimbabwe celebrates the existence of two annual conferences, someone still has to deal with a number of unanswered questions. One such question is Who makes the African M*ufundisi*, or Pastor? Why did it take such a long time for the African preachers to climb the ministerial institutional tree? They started as native helpers, then native pastor-teachers. Then they became deacons, and finally, they were approved to become elders. What a long journey! Why? Again, who makes the African M*ufundisi*? There are a number of factors that come together toward the making of *mufundisi*, and I shall discuss them in this chapter.

African Titles of M*ufundisi*

The title *mufundisi*, which the Methodist Episcopal Church adapted as their title for pastor in Southern Rhodesia, has its roots in the church's historical background with church traditions in both Portuguese and South Africa. The term *mufundisi* must have come from outside Southern Rhodesia, since Methodism was in both South Africa and Portuguese East Africa before it came to Southern Rhodesia. From our theology students at Africa University I learned that:

(a) The Zulu people in South Africa and the Ndebele people in Zimbabwe call their pastor *umfundisi*, meaning both teacher and pastor.
(b) The Shangani people in Mozambique call their pastor *mufundisi*, meaning both teacher and pastor.
(c) The Xitswa people in Mozambique call their pastor *murisi*, meaning teacher.
(d) The Kimbundu people of central Angola call their pastor *mesene*, meaning master or teacher.
(e) The Luba people of the Democratic Republic of Congo call their pastor *mufundishi*, meaning teacher.

(f) In West Nigeria the Hausa call their pastor *ma'aikachin ubangiji*, meaning teacher.
(g) In the eastern region of the Democratic Republic of Congo where Swahili is widely used they call their pastor *mutsungaji*, meaning a shepherd.
(h) In the southern region of the Democratic Republic of Congo they use *mutsahungaji*, meaning shepherd.
(i) In the western region of the Democratic of Congo the Lingala people call their pastor *mukambi*, meaning shepherd.
(j) In Zimbabwe the Shona people call their pastor *mufundisi*, literally meaning teacher.

The majority of the annual conferences of The United Methodist Church in Africa use different titles for pastor, but the titles primarily bear two meanings—teacher and shepherd. Those who have an African title for *mufundisi*, meaning shepherd, seem to be more faithful to the original meaning of the term *pastor*, which in the New Testament Greek is *poimen* (Matt. 9:36; John 10:2, 12), meaning a shepherd. Those who interpret *mufundisi* to mean teacher are faithful to the literal meaning for the term. Indeed, *mufundisi* or *umfundi* or *mufundishi* literally mean teacher. This may have come about because it was *mufundisi* who brought both education and the gospel to the African villages. There is no doubt that many people responded to the gospel for education more than for anything else. Thus, the pastor was perceived more as a teacher than a shepherd.

As much as the Gospels present Jesus as a preacher of the good news (Mark 1:14; Matt. 4:23; Luke 4:16), the same Gospels also portray him as a *rabbi* (John 1:49; 20:16) or teacher (John 11:28; Matt. 4:23; 22:36) who taught "as one who had authority" (Mark 1:22; Matt. 7:29). He accepted the title *teacher* when he said to his disciples, "You call me 'Teacher' " (John 13:13), and he taught them often. According to the

Gospel of John, Jesus also attributed to himself the title *the good shepherd* (John 10:11), who not only knew his sheep, but also laid down his life for the sheep. His parable of the lost sheep (Luke 15:1–7) portrays the passion of a good shepherd for the sheep. The vocation or ministry of African pastors of The United Methodist Church in Zimbabwe, which was begun by humble native helpers who later on were called pastor-teachers, developed into a powerful institution, and those who participate in it are called by the rich and inclusive term *mufundisi*. It does not matter whether one is ordained or not ordained, male or female, old or young, black or white. As long as one is a preacher, teacher, or shepherd, one is called *mufundisi* by the church, even by the world.

Divine Calling

African Christians have never questioned the fact that God calls God's people. This is partly due to their understanding of African communal life, where ancestors return to the realm of the living and may ask whoever is favoured to perform certain functions, either for the family, clan, or an ethnic group. What African Christians may want to know is whether God's calling is different from that of the ancestors. If so, how different is it? In answering this question I begin by saying there are two types of divine calling.

First, there is a calling for everybody to God's salvation. It was the Lord God who first called to Adam, "Where are you?" (Gen. 3:9). The biblical drama from the book of Genesis to Revelation is one story of God and humankind—the story of God's salvation for humankind. God has been calling ever since, and God continues calling us to salvation to this day. Indeed, the early Christians understood the concept of calling primarily as divine calling or call to God's salvation. That is the message early Christians seem to share with us in the following scriptures: Romans 8:30, 11:28; 1 Corinthians 1:16, 7:20; Ephesians 1:18, 4:1, 4; Philippians 3:14; 2 Thessalonians 1:11; 2 Timothy 1:9; Hebrews 3:1; and 2 Peter 1:10. This is the message we receive in reading the parables that Jesus taught: the parable of the Great Banquet (Matt. 22:2–14; Luke 14:15–24); parable of the Lost Sheep (Matt. 18:12–14; Luke 15:1–7); parable of the Lost Coin (Luke 15:8–10); parable of the Lost Son (Luke 15:11–32), and others. In other words, everyone becomes Christian because he or she responds to the call of God through his Son Jesus Christ. It is important for pastors to remember that according to the early church every church member who confessed Jesus Christ as Saviour and Lord was responding to God's call.

It is not only those who have responded positively who are called. The gospel of God's grace teaches us that all people are called to salvation, but there are some who turn down the offer (Luke 14:18), or who would rather hang on to their way of life (Matt. 19:22)—people who choose not to have their lives changed. Such was the man Jesus looked at and loved so much, but after asking him to sell everything he had and follow him, the man turned down the offer (Mark 10:21f). That one biblical story by Mark represents the stories of thousands to this day who turn down the offer of salvation. So, a calling to salvation is first a call to everybody, and that divine call can either be accepted or rejected.

Second, God does not call a people or person to salvation without showing that person God's mission at the same time. While salvation is attained in our willingness to be in a special relationship with God, the same God also calls God's people to be involved in God's mission. Jesus made that point clearly when he said to his disciples, "Whoever wants to become great among you must be your servant, and whoever wants to be first must be slave of all" (Mark 10:43–44). God, through God's Son, makes people God's servants, or slaves. In other words, the object of God's calling a person is not to make an individual great, but that one comes into a redemptive relationship with God, and that one becomes God's servant (*diakonos*—helper, minister, deacon, deaconess). Neither does God call a person to be first among humankind, but to become God's slave (*doulos*—servant).[216] Paul understood that new relationship after his encounter with the risen Christ on the road to Damascus, calling himself "a servant of Christ Jesus" (Rom. 1:1; Phil. 1:1).

We have often associated this divine calling with packing our bags and going into the ordained ministry. That is not the whole truth. Every Christian has received a call, not only to salvation, but also to the kind of ministry God wants him or her to do. God is always calling God's people for a *diakonia*—"ministry, service, contribution, help, support, mission; perhaps office of deacon or authority."[217] This calling is not just for ordained ministers, it is for all Christians, and each Christian finds fulfillment of the heart's desire when they discover what God has for them as a life vocation, as Paul says:

> We have different gifts, according to the grace given us. If a man's gift is prophesying, let him use it in proportion to his faith. If it is serving, let him serve; if it is teaching, let him teach; if it is encouraging, let him encourage; if it is contributing to the needs of others, let him give generously; if it is leadership, let him govern diligently; if it is showing mercy, let him do it cheerfully. (Rom. 12:6–8)

Again, in the letter to the Ephesians, we read:

> It was he who gave some to be apostles, some to be prophets, some to be evangelists, and some to be pastors and teachers, to prepare God's people for . . . service, so that the body of Christ may be built up until we all reach unity in the faith and in the knowledge of the Son of God and become mature, attaining to the whole measure of the fullness of Christ. (Eph. 4:11–13)

For too long, the clergy have monopolized the claim of divine calling at the exclusion of the laity. God called Abraham to salvation as God asked him to leave his own country, his people, and his father's house to go to the Promised Land (Gen. 12:1). God did not call Abraham to be a preacher but to be in a special relationship with God—a relationship that enabled Abraham to become a servant patriarch, and from him to make a great nation for both his own salvation and God's salvation of humankind. Moses was called not to be a preacher but a servant leader for the children (Exod. 3:1–22); neither was David called to be a preacher, but king of Israel (1 Sam. 16:13). This is the same God who called Amos (Amos 7:10–16), Isaiah (Isa. 6:1–13); Jeremiah (Jer. 1:4–8)–and many other prophets to proclaim God's will to the people of Israel. Through God's Son, Jesus, God called the twelve to be apostles: Mark (Mark 1:14–20; 2:13–17; 3:13–19), Matthew (Matt. 10:2–4; Luke 6:14–16), and Paul (Gal. 1:11–24; Acts 9:1–19). No one is called simply to salvation; rather we are all called to salvation and commissioned to God's mission. Either immediately or gradually, it dawns on us.

To this day, the same God who does not change (Heb. 13:8) continues calling people to salvation, while at the same time creating a relationship in which all those who are called and who accept the calling are made God's servants for the whole of humankind. Thus, some are called to be preachers of the Word, so that people know the truth about life; others are called to be teachers of children and adults alike. Others are called to be agriculturists—to feed people and nations; still others are called to be health workers. Some are called to be businessmen and businesswomen to provide material supplies necessary for life; others are called to many other professions. The point is that a person who is called to salvation and enters into a relationship with God becomes conscious of what God wants him or her to do as a servant of God. In paraphrasing Paul's words, that is the person who is likely to say, "Woe to me if I do not" do what God called me to (1 Cor. 9:16).

As we look back over our lives, we know of great teachers, health workers, and many other laypersons who were dedicated to their work.

The unfortunate thing was the clergy monopolized a theology of calling, and those dedicated laypersons, servants of God, were never told that they were also the called servants of God. The United Methodist Church is increasingly coming closer to this understanding of divine calling for everybody, and is now commissioning laypersons to God's *diaconia* or service. United Methodist Church ordination now includes those ordained as elders for the ordained ministry, deacons, who "are called by God to a lifetime of servant leadership, authorized by the Church, ordained by a bishop,"[218] while at the same time serving full-time in another profession. But we need to continue moving on to an inclusive theology, which affirms that all people are called into a relationship with God, and that it is the same God who gives some to be preachers, some to be teachers, some to be carpenters, some to be agriculturalists, some to be businessmen or businesswomen, some to be politicians, and all working for the common good for all humanity or the world that God so loved (John 3:16).

The Church Makes *Mufundisi*

Often the question is raised, Who makes *mufundisi*? Is it the church or the theological institution? Or is it both? First, I would like to assert that the church makes *mufundisi*. A few years ago, when I was a student of theology at Hartzell Theological Seminary, we used to go to the Hilltop United Methodist Church once every week for a class in homiletics. The lecturer was Josiah Chimbadzwa, one of the best preachers of his time in our conference. As we went to class one morning, we met one of the elderly pastors of The United Methodist Church, whose rural church was not far from the city of Mutare. One of the students engaged in a daring discussion with the pastor.

"Pastor, we see you in town almost all the time we are here! Tell us, when do you do your pastoral work?" the student rudely asked.

"What work do you talk about?" responded the pastor.

"I mean pastoral work. Don't you do some pastoral visitation, since you have about seven churches in your circuit? That is a lot of work that takes a lot of time going round, doesn't it?" the student explained.

"This is where you young pastors are wrong!" the pastor replied. "You young pastors coming out of the seminary these days spend a lot of time visiting people in their homes, even in their fields, disturbing their working routine, which is not the case with us. You are spoiling these congregations. In our time, if people needed the pastor they knew where to find him. They came to see the pastor at the main church of the circuit or parsonage. Some people waited for a day or two if they had come from an out-station, if they really needed to see the pastor," the elderly pastor explained.

Maybe this problem is partly explained by a compliment to young pastors of today that my mother, in her 90s, gave a few years before her death. As one who could not easily walk to church, she was impressed by a young pastor who had just been appointed to her circuit. So she said to me, "The pastors of today are very different from the pastors we had about forty or fifty years ago." I was keen to listen as one who had been involved in the training of today's pastors.

"The young pastors of today show concern for people, especially the sick and the elderly people in the villages. They make pastoral calls in every home, and they bring communion to the shut-ins," she said. "That was not the case during our time," she added.

"Was it not because during your time pastors were few in number with circuits to look after?" I asked.

"That could be true also," she agreed with me. But she went on to say, "During my time the early pastors in our circuits did not visit people in the homes; instead the people visited them, and took food, such as pounded maize meal mealie, vegetables, and at times meat to give to the pastor."

I asked, "Why was it so?"

"I think it was because most of those early pastors came from chieftainship families. They were chiefs and expected people to pay them visits, instead of the other way around. Hence, the church members often considered and addressed those pastors who came from chieftainship families not just as pastors, but also as chiefs or sons of chiefs. That was the reason pastors did not visit in the homes the way the young pastors of today do," my mother explained.

When one begins to count the number of pastors, especially in the Methodist Episcopal Church in Southern Rhodesia, who came from chieftainship families, the explanation seems to make sense. Indeed, it was the chiefs who first sent their sons and daughters to mission schools and many of them became pastor-teachers and even pastors. Interestingly enough, the elderly pastor that my seminarian encountered was from a chieftainship family and had begun his ministry before the 1920s. He was a child of his era, whose church had picked up the African cultural ethos that made him the kind of *mufundisi* he became.

Yes, *mufundisi* is made by the church, and should be molded in and through the church. But the culture also colours the church in which *mufundisi* is molded. Theologically speaking, *mufundisi* comes "from within the community of faith and not to it from the outside."[219] He or she is one of the baptized members of the community, who is now set aside for the pastoral ministry of preaching, teaching the Word, healing persons and communities, and administering the sacraments of the Church of Jesus Christ. It is the church that confirms that one from among them is being called to the ordained ministry as a vocation. The church gives the individual candidate opportunities for leadership among them to satisfy themselves in their assessment. The church often shows its support for the candidate for ministry by casting their vote in approval, through prayer and material support for further theological training. Thus, *the church makes mufundisi*.

Second, theological institutions train *vafundisi* (plural). Theological institutions that train *vafundisi* are known by various names, such as bible school, theological seminary, theological college. In universities, such theological training happens within departments of religious studies or under faculty of theology. These theological institutions play a significant role in molding the African pastors that we see in the African churches today. But, what is their significant role or task? Thomas Long makes an important point:

> Seminaries are sometimes jokingly called "preacher factories," as if it were the task of theological schools to take the people and fabricate them into ministers. This is not the case at all. Ministers are not made in seminaries. Seminaries train ministers; ministers are made in and through the church. People come to seminaries to gain deeper knowledge of the Christian story, but they were first taught that story by the Christian people in the church. They come to seminary to acquire the skills of guiding, teaching, counseling, and speaking, but they come because the church, in some way, has already discerned in them gifts for leadership. They leave seminary not to create the church but to take their places of service in its ongoing ministry.[220]

For example, Candler School of Theology at Emory University, Atlanta, Georgia (USA), began a Teaching Parish Program for their students in the mid-1970s. The main purpose of this programme is to integrate experiential and theoretical learning for the student. It aims to afford every student the opportunity to participate in contextual education, which is provided by the church and society, and to gain new academic biblical, historical, theological, and religious insights in classroom lectures. For example, while first-year students may meet with a United Methodist elder for a total of twenty hours per semester as part of their supervision, they will meet for a total of six hours each semester with their Faculty Advisor. This shows that there is a strong realization that it is the church that makes *mufundisi*; or that the blazing furnace in which ministers are molded is in the life of the church itself.

Augustine, Bishop of Hippo, recognised the relationship between the church and the making of *mufundisi*, and was the first bishop to establish a cathedral monastery "in which study and church administration were combined"[221] for the training of priests. He discovered the weakness in the system where priests were trained in the monastery distinctly away from the daily happenings of church life. Theology students need to be afforded the opportunity to experience church life and rub shoulders with the leading pastors of churches where their institution is located—be it in the classroom, Bible study, or the pulpit. Our theological institutions may want to restore theological education and training back into the life-stream of the church. Theological institutions should not be viewed as outside the church; there is need for a closer working relationship between the church and theological institutions to participate in the making of pastors for "preachers come from within the church, not to it from the outside."[222]

Third, who provides models for the African *mufundisi* in training? Is it a lecturer or professor who is teaching him or her in the classroom or a pastor already out in the field? I am intrigued by the way medical doctors and nurses are trained and the way they practice their vocation. A teaching hospital is central to the training of doctors and nurses. Often, even if medical specialists teach in medical training institutions, they remain attached either to a hospital where they may be specialists or to their private surgery where clients are referred to them. Africa University introduced a Faculty of Health Sciences in 2003 with "a Graduate Certificate Programme in Community Health, and a Post Basic Bachelors Degree (B.Sc.) in Nursing."[223] The following training centres had long been lined up for the clinical training for the nurses: the sixty-bed Old Mutare United Methodist Hospital, the two-hundred-bed Government Hospital in Mutare, and community health training at the Primary Health Centres.[224] The teaching hospital often is equipped with expensive equipment, making it the focal ground for teaching and learning experiences. It is the context in which doctors under training and nurses are made. The teaching doctors who meet students in the teaching hospital—both in the classroom and operating theatre—become the model for those young women and men who aspire to be doctors or even specialists.

So, who provides these models for the African pastor? Those who study for a degree or diploma in theology have left their churches for a theological institution that will teach them theory about the ministry for three or four years. Chances are that not all the scholars charged with the responsibility to train these candidates, unlike the system for training doctors, are practicing pastors or currently appointed to a charge or circuit as pastor. A professor in a faculty of theology, or any teacher in any theological institution, has difficulties taking students into real church-life situations where the church is worshipping, holding a board meeting, planning a church budget, involved in group counseling, or leading a revival meeting, and where he or she is the practitioner. As such, students do not see their lecturers or professors as practicing pastors. A professor may preach in local churches once in a while, may present papers, conduct workshops, and other good ministerial duties, but still is not a practicing pastor in a local church setting.

These theological institutions may attempt to close the gap between themselves and the local churches by hiring a director of fieldwork. He or she is charged with seeing that all that is taught in the institution, from biblical, historical, theological, church and society, and ministerial studies, is practically applied by the students. This system dichotomizes theological education and training or the classroom and applied learning. We inherited this system from western theological institutions, and it has worked well for those institutions that have the resources to support their systems. But I still raise the question, Who provides the model for our students when it comes to the pastoral ministry?

On 8 November 2002, the Faculty of Theology at Africa University conducted a workshop for pastors who were to supervise our students' fieldwork. During the ensuing discussion, one of the pastors hit the nail on the head when he asked, "So as supervisors, we will be the role models for the students?" In contrast to what is happening in the established churches, at times I find that an assistant bank manager or a company manager is a pastor of a fast-growing church in town. I asked where they received their theological education and training. The answer was that the senior pastor of such a fast-growing church, with the assistance of a few other pastors, manages theological education and training for all their pastors. They conduct evening and weekend classes for pastors, and separately for laity, for various positions. They may also send their pastors for training to a theological institution for short periods, from a month up to six months. The pastor in charge becomes the model for those under training. Although more extensive theological education and training may be needed, there is a mutual relationship between the church and the training institutions. Further, the young men and women in training regard their senior pastor as their model for ministry of the church. This is one approach to theological education and training of ministerial training for a growing church in Africa.

Henry Mitchell is an African-American preacher and scholar who has authored numerous books on preaching and has written with great profundity. We need to examine and take heed of Mitchell's critique of our current approach to theological education and training:

> I'm the director of a center out in Los Angeles, called the Ecumenical Center for Black Church Studies. Perhaps the most important difference between us and any other institution for theological training is not so much what we study in terms of a particular group of people, but the fact that we want at every point to have professors who are

> also pastors. We do not want to train people who all the rest of their lives are identifying with professors and aspiring to professorship, rather than identifying with pastors, aspiring to be shepherds of the flock—aspiring above all to serve laity. You cannot sit where they sit if you've always got your eye off somewhere on a professorship. All too many people have been misfit because that's really what they've been programmed for.[225]

That is the message that Paul passed on to the church of Thessalonica; that he, Silas, and Timothy had modeled for them "like a caring mother for her little children" (1 Thess. 2:7); that they had "worked night and day in order not to be a burden to anyone while we preached the gospel of God to you" (1 Thess. 2:9). Paul constantly elaborated on how he and his team had modeled for the church with their leadership what it meant to follow Christ. They did all that, not because they did not have the right to receive support from the church, "but in order to make ourselves a model for you to follow" (2 Thess. 3:9). I support Henry Mitchell's view that the professor or lecturer in a theological institution may not be the best model for the African theology student aspiring to be a pastor. No wonder most of our students who go to America to study do not become pastors when they come home, but lecturers and professors in academic institutions such as Africa University. We need good lecturers. But we also need leaders who will model for our students who aspire to be pastors in Africa. It may be difficult to serve as a model of something you are not doing or have not done. Like in the medical training programme, we need to accept that: (a) *mufundisi* is made in and through the church; (b) as Augustine of Hippo realized, *mufundisi* must be trained within the contextual education of the life of the church, and (c) we must look to pastors, not lecturers or professors, as models for our future African preachers.

Chapter 10

Conclusion and Recommendations

In African tradition, elderly people do not often ask a young man or woman his or her name as a way of introduction. Rather, they ask, "Whose son or daughter are you?" They do so because by knowing the parents or generations of grandparents they already know the kind of person they meet. That is precisely what Eugen Rosenstock-Huessy meant when he said, "The true past points into the future."[226]

The conclusion of this book summarizes the issues explored in its chapters in an effort to show that African leaders, though originally called native helpers, were in the forefront of propagating the gospel and planting churches, especially in the villages. I will also make some recommendations for how this book may be used in the life of the church.

First, we noted that Methodism's evangelism in Africa was begun by North American freed slaves who returned to Africa. In 1819, John Stewart, the son of a freed slave, aroused the formation of the Missionary Society of the Methodist Episcopal Church. Daniel Coker, an ordained preacher of the African Methodist Episcopal Church, together with other freed slaves, introduced Episcopal Methodism to Africa, by way of Liberia in 1822. The first missionary of the Methodist Episcopal Church, Melville Cox, arrived in Liberia in 1833. We noted that the Liberia Conference was administered from America, as it was part of the racially divided Black Central Conference system in the United States. Bishop William Taylor (1884–96) was the first resident missionary bishop for Africa, and was responsible for opening Methodist Episcopal Church work in countries such as Angola, Belgium Congo, and Portuguese East Africa. He supervised work in Liberia, which was already an annual conference, and the work outside Liberia, known as the Congo Mission Conference. Bishop Taylor's legacy stems not only from his commitment to evangelization and mission in Africa, but from his insistence that the church in Africa must be indigenous and self-supporting, a principle and promise that must guide us still today.

Second, Bishop Joseph Crane Hartzell, who served from 1896 until 1916, was a man led by a vision to establish Methodist Episcopal Church work in Southern Africa under the British flag. His dream was fulfilled when he was granted Old Mutare—an abandoned site where the town of Mutare had been located. That site was granted on two conditions: (1) that the Methodist Episcopal Church establish a school for European children in Mutare; and (2) that the same Church establish an industrial mission for the African children at Old Mutare Mission. The conditions were fulfilled. One lasting result is the pivotal role Old Mutare Mission has played in the development of The United Methodist Church in Zimbabwe, educating scores of Zimbabwean leaders for roles in church and in society for several generations.

Third, by an act of the 1900 General Conference of the Methodist Episcopal Church that met in Chicago, two mission conferences were formed from the Congo Mission Conference: (1) The East Central Africa Mission Conference that included the work in East Africa south of the equator; and (2) The West Central Africa Mission Conference that included the work in West Africa south of the equator. The East Central Africa Mission Conference was convened at the call of Bishop Hartzell and held its first session at St. Andrew, then the chapel of the Mutare Academy, in Mutare 16–25 November 1901.

It is important to note that there were at least two Africans present at the creation of the first mission conference in the region. One was Tizore M. Navess, an African pastor of the Makodweni Church on the Inhambane District, from Portuguese East Africa. Navess actually was pastor of the Makodweni Episcopal Church, but since he was not ordained, he was considered only a helper. The other was George Muponda from Southern Rhodesia, a layman and teacher at the Mutare African Methodist Episcopal Church. It was at this first mission conference session that sharing testimonies became a fundamental characteristic of a Methodist.

Fourth, chapters 4, 5, and 6 show the number of both missionaries and African pastor-teachers who were involved in the spreading of the gospel. If the missionaries were strategists who provided the supplies, the African pastors were responsible for penetrating the African villages and towns to share the gospel and to establish preaching points wherever they went. Their impact is evident in how often we Zimbabwean readers come across familiar family names in these chapters, even though we may not know the individuals concerned.

Finally, chapters 7, 8, and 9 show the historical journey that the African pastor has traveled in search of a new identity, and his or her rightful position in the life of The United Methodist Church and it predecessors (Methodist Episcopal Church and Methodist Church). It has been a long journey. Some pastor-teachers started as domestic servants and garden boys in the missionaries's homes, where they received their recommendation to become preachers of the gospel. Others were lucky enough to start their vocational journey from the classroom, either because they were sons and daughters of chiefs who requested that the missionaries educate their children or they were identified and handpicked by missionaries from the villages they visited.

As soon as they became local preachers, some of them were appointed to look after a circuit as native helpers. Later, they were identified as pastor-teachers. Those were the people who, while at Old Mutare Mission for pastors' school in June 1918, God blessed with a spiritual renewal to become a new people. They realized in that renewal experience that the same God who had called the missionaries to cross the oceans to Africa had called them from their various villages to preach the gospel.

We noted that only one pastor-teacher qualified to be ordained a deacon in 1921—the first one after twenty years of history of the Methodist Episcopal Church in Southern Rhodesia, and four were ordained elders in 1929. That was a milestone on the journey of faith for the Methodist Episcopal Church in Rhodesia, and a great personal achievement of the individual deacons and elders.

Today, ordination for an elder in The United Methodist Church in the Zimbabwe Episcopal Area takes a minimum of three years in a theological institution, and two years in service under the bishop's appointment. Despite the achievements of the orders, the questions continue to be asked: Who makes the Africa Pastor? Is the African Pastor truly made in the classroom or by the church? How do we combine the classroom experience with the modeling that must come from mature African pastors? What can we learn and gain today from the pastor-teacher model and its benefits? What are the best models of an African Pastor, and who can serve as those models?

Recommendations for Using This Book in the Life of Local Churches

This book is written for the church and can be utilized in a number of creative ways, both directly and indirectly, to enrich our people's appreciation for who we are as Methodists in Africa.

First, the book could be used as a study book by various groups of the local churches or circuits—groups such as Bible study groups, *Vabvuwi* (Men's Organization), *Rukwadzano* (Women's Organization), and the youth of The United Methodist Church—so that they know the history of their church.

Knowing or not knowing our history has consequences. A few years ago, prior to creation of the two annual conferences, Zimbabwe East Annual Conference and Zimbabwe West Annual Conference, there was a heated debate on the conference floor about the legitimacy of dividing a conference in two. People had forgotten the recorded history in our journals that show that the Congo Mission Conference was divided to form two mission conferences in 1901, and that in 1915 the East Central Africa Mission Conference was divided to create the Inhambane Mission Conference and the Rhodesia Mission Conference. Members of our Church—both clergy and laity—need to know the history of their church. This book serves to fulfill that need.

Second, the book could be used as resource material for Sunday school lessons. There are a good number of our Christians who associate the origin of Episcopal Methodism in Africa only with the white missionaries. As important as the white missionaries have been, it is time to get the message straight across the church that it was the African freed slaves who first brought the gospel to Africa.

Third, African United Methodism needs to learn to celebrate the heroic lives of some of its pioneering African leaders, both clergy and laity. There are certain personalities, including both Africans and missionaries, whose photographs could be made available to our local churches. Those people played a significant role in laying the foundation of the Methodist Episcopal Church in Belgium Congo, Liberia, Portuguese East Africa, Southern Rhodesia, and other countries; they need to be recognized by the church.

Likewise, the African pastor-teachers who lived and laboured between 1901 and 1921 in Southern Rhodesia, most of whom are gone, have not received sufficient recognition by the living of today. Those are the people who penetrated the villages with the gospel. They preached from Friday evening through Sunday, and from Monday morning to Friday noon they were in the classroom, teaching three to five classes. Their witness lives with us. Many of the churches that we find in rural Africa today are a result of their labour; they are the ones who planted them. Someone must tell their story.

Finally, this book could serve as Christian education material in class meetings or sections. It could provide teachers with content for Sunday school lessons and confirmation lessons.

The members of our local churches need to understand the history of their church. Certainly, that understanding begins with knowing the foundational stories and struggles of the early church through the Gospels, in Acts, and in the Pauline and Pastoral Epistles. It continues as we learn of our linkages to a distinctive set of Christians called Methodists, the spiritual legacy of John and Charles Wesley, and the growth of Methodist movement in Great Britain and in America. But our understanding is incomplete, and our vision as well, until we see how Methodism not only came to Africa but became African, even Zimbabwean. Understanding our history as a church allows us to claim the ways God has worked in and through Africans to plant and grow the church here and to enrich the Methodist movement with our stories and our character.

Bibliography

Africa University Prospectus (2003–2005)

T. A. Beetham, *Christianity in the New Africa* (London: Pall Mall Press, 1967)

Thomas D. Blakely, Walter E. A. van Beek, Dennis L. Thomson, eds. *Religion in Africa: Experience and Expression* (London: James Currey, 1994)

The Book of Discipline of The United Methodist Church, Africa Central Conference Edition, 1988 (1990)

John Calvin, *A Compend of the Institutes of the Christian Religion*, ed. Hugh T. Kerr (Philadelphia: The Westminster Press, 1939)

The Christian as Minister (Nashville: United Methodist General Board of Higher Education, 1997)

J. Tremayne Copplestone, *History of Methodist Missions*, Vol. IV (New York: The Board of Global Ministries of The United Methodist Church, 1973)

Bart D. Ehrman, *The New Testament* (Oxford: Oxford University Press, 2000)

Faculty of Health Sciences: Africa University, "General and Historical Statement of Methodist Episcopal Mission in East Central Africa," ECAMC, 1901

G. S. P. Freeman-Grenville, *The New Atlas of African History* (New York: Simon and Schuster, 1991)

Joseph C. Hartzell, *The African Mission of the Episcopal Church* (February 1909)

The History of American Methodism, Vol. I & II, (Nashville: Abingdon Press, 1964)

The Interpreter's Dictionary of the Bible, A–D (1962)

Henry I. James, *Missions in Rhodesia Under The Methodist Episcopal Church* (Old Mutare: Rhodesia Press, 1935)

Journal of the East Central Africa Mission Conference, of the Methodist Episcopal Church, 1901–1912

John Wesley Z. Kurewa, *The Church in Mission: A Short History of the United Methodist Church in Zimbabwe*, 1897–1997) (Nashville: Abingdon Press,1997)

Kenneth Scott Latourette, *A History of Christianity* (New York: Harper & Row, 1953)

Umphrey Lee and William Warren Sweet, *A Short History of Methodism* (Nashville: Abingdon Press, 1956)

Thomas G. Long, *The Witness of Preaching* (Louisville: W/JK Press, 1989)

Minutes of the Rhodesia Mission Conference of the Methodist Episcopal Church (1917–1925)

Minutes of the East Central Africa Mission Conference (1901–1925)

"The Mission Extension of the United Methodist Church in Africa," *Umbowo* (October 1972)

Henry H. Mitchell, *The Recovery of Preaching* (San Francisco: Harper & Row, 1977)

Stephen Neill, *A History of Christian Missions* (Penguin Books, 1964)

Barclay M. Newman, *A Concise Greek-English Dictionary of the New Testament* (London: United Bible Societies, 1971)

Frederick Perry Noble, *The Redemption of Africa: A Story of Civilization* (New York: Fleming H. Revel Company, 1819)

Frederick A. Norwood, *The Story of American Methodism* (Nashville: Abingdon Press, 1974)

Thomas C. Oden, *Pastoral Theology* (New York: Harper & Row, Publishers, 1983)

Official Journal of the Rhodesia Annual Conference (1936)

Roland Oliver and J. D. Fage, *A Short History of Africa*, 6th ed. (New York: Penguin Books, 1990)

George Abbott-Smith, *A Manual Greek Lexicon of the New Testament* (Edinburgh: T & T Clark, 1968)

William Taylor, *The Story of My Life* (New York: Hunt and Eaton, 1986)

F. Thomas Trotter, *Loving God with One's Mind* (Nashville: The Board of Higher Education and Ministry of The United Methodist Church, 1987)

The Works of John Wesley (1872)

Edward Krusen Ziegler, *The Village Pastor* (New York: Agricultural Missions, Inc., 1959)

Endnotes

1. Harvey J. Sindima, *Drums of Redemption* (London: Praeger, 1999).
2. F. F. Bruce, *Commentary on the Book of The Acts* (Grand Rapids: William B. Eerdmans, 1966), 190.
3. *The Works of John Wesley*, Vol. 2, 464.
4. Ibid.
5. Frederick Perry Noble, *The Redemption of Africa: A Story of Civilization* (New York: Fleming H. Revel, 1819), 304.
6. Umphrey Lee and William Warren Sweet, *A Short History of Methodism* (Nashville: Abingdon Press, 1956), 65f.
7. Ibid.
8. Ibid., 66.
9. Ibid.
10. *The History of American Methodism*, Vol. I (Nashville: Abingdon Press, 1964), 605.
11. Ibid.
12. *The Book of Discipline of The United Methodist Church, Africa Central Conference Edition*, 1988 (1990), 3.
13. Noble, *The Redemption of Africa*, 305.
14. Ibid.
15. Ibid., 306.
16. Ibid.
17. *The History of American Methodism*, Vol. II, 621.
18. Ibid., 610.
19. Ibid.
20. Ibid., 621.
21. Ibid.
22. Ibid.
23. Frederick A. Norwood, *The Story of American Methodism* (Nashville: Abingdon Press, 1974), 298.
24. Ibid., 311.
25. Kenneth Scott Latourette, *A History of Christianity* (New York: Harper & Row, 1953), 1317.
26. Noble, *The Redemption of Africa*, 309.
27. Ibid., 313.
28. Ibid., 310.
29. ECAMC (1901), 21.
30. Ibid.
31. John W. Z. Kurewa, *The Church in Mission* (Nashville: Abingdon Press, 1987), 20.

32. Noble, *The Redemption of Africa*, 313.
33. Ibid.
34. Stephen Neill, *A History of Christian Missions* (New York: Penguin Books, 1964), 259.
35. William Taylor, *The Story of My Life* (New York: Hunt and Eaton, 1886), 696.
36. ECAMC (1901), 25.
37. Ibid.
38. Ibid.
39. Norwood, *The Story of American Methodism*, 339.
40. J. Tremayne Copplestone, *History of Methodist Missions*, Vol. IV (New York: The Board of Global Ministries of The United Methodist Church, 1973), 3.
41. Roland Oliver and J. D. Page, *A Short History of Africa*, 6th ed., (New York: Penguin Books, 1990), 165.
42. ECAMC (1901), VIf.
43. Ibid., VII.
44. Ibid.
45. Ibid., VIf.
46. Noble, *The Redemption of Africa*, 311.
47. Joseph C. Hartzell, *The African Mission of the Episcopal Church* (1909), 46.
48. ECAMC (1913), VII.
49. Ibid., VII.
50. Ibid.
51. Henry I. James, *Mission in Rhodesia Under The Methodist Episcopal Church* (Old Mutare: Rhodesia Mission Press, 1935), viii.
52. ECAMC (1913), 7.
53. Ibid.
54. Ibid.
55. ECAMC (1901), VIII.
56. ECAMC (1913), 8.
57. ECAMC (1901), VIII.
58. *The Book of Discipline of The United Methodist Church, Africa Central Conference Edition* (1990), 4.
59. Ibid.
60. ECAMC (1901), 6.
61. Ibid.
62. Ibid.
63. Ibid., VI.
64. Ibid., VIII.
65. Ibid., 12.
66. Ibid., 44.
67. Ibid., 17f.
68. *The Works of John Wesley* (1872), 340f.
69. Ibid., 341.
70. ECAMC (1901), 9.

71. ECAMC (1901), 35f.
72. Ibid., 42f.
73. Ibid., 58.
74. Ibid.
75. Ibid., 12.
76. Thomas D. Blakely, Walter E. A. van Beek and Dennis L. Thomson, eds., *Religion in Africa* (London: James Currey, 1994), 280.
77. ECAMC (1903), 20f.
78. Ibid., 21f.
79. Ibid.
80. Ibid.
81. ECAMC (1912), 15.
82. Ibid., 19.
83. Kurewa, *The Church in Mission*, 52.
84. ECAMC (1903), 22.
85. Ibid., 29.
86. Ibid., (1905), 17.
87. Ibid., 1907 (1908), 26.
88. Ibid.
89. Ibid.
90. Ibid.
91. Ibid., (1930), 30.
92. Ibid., (1905), 18.
93. ECAMC (1905), 18.
94. Ibid.
95. Ibid., (1909), 34.
96. Ibid., (1905), 17.
97. Ibid., (1907), 24.
98. Ibid., (1909), 60.
99. Ibid.
100. ECAMC (1905), 18.
101. Ibid._
102. Ibid. (1907), 44.
103. Ibid., 25.
104. Ibid., 1907 (1908), 28.
105. Ibid. (1909), 35.
106. Ibid. (1909), 35.
107. Ibid., 36.
108. Ibid., 36.
109. Ibid. (1909), 37.
110. Ibid., 22.
111. Ibid. (1910), 65.
112. Ibid. (1907), 25.

113. Ibid. (1907), 25.
114. Ibid.
115. Ibid., 27.
116. Ibid.
117. Ibid. 1907 (1908), 51
118. MRMC (1919), 30.
119. Ibid. (1907), 48.
120. Ibid, 1907, (1908), 49.
121. ECAMC (1911), 51.
122. Ibid., 51.
123. ECAMC (1901), VIII.
124. Ibid., V.
125. Ibid.
126. Ibid. (1901), VIII.
127. Ibid.
128. ECAMC (1909), 32.
129. Ibid. (1901), VIII.
130. Ibid.
131. Ibid., V.
132. Ibid., V.
133. Ibid. (1905), 26f.
134. ECAMC (1901), V.
135. Ibid. (1903), 21.
136. Ibid. (1905), 24.
137. Ibid., 28.
138. Ibid. (1907), 24.
139. Ibid., 24.
140. ECAMC (1901), 15.
141. Ibid., 22.
142. Ibid. (1909), 40f.
143. Kurewa, *The Church in Mission*, 98.
144. ECAMC (1907), 34.
145. Ibid., 34.
146. Ibid., 22.
147. Ibid.
148. Ibid. (1905), 20.
149. Ibid. (1907), 40.
150. ECAMC (1909), 54.
151. Ibid.
152. Ibid. (1910), 36.
153. ECAMC 1907 (1908), 43.
154. ECAMC (1907), 31.
155. Ibid., 1907 (1908), 41.
156. John Wesley Z. Kurewa, *The Church in Mission* (Nashville: Abingdon Press, 1997), 96.

157. ECAMC, 1907 (1908), 41.
158. Ibid.
159. Ibid. (1907), 31f.
160. Ibid., 51.
161. Ibid. (1909), 51.
162. Ibid.
163. Ibid. (1910), 50.
164. Ibid.
165. Ibid., 50f.
166. Ibid. (1910), 51.
167. Ibid., 52.
168. Ibid. (1911), 27.
169. Ibid. (1910), 52f.
170. Ibid. (1917), 57.
171. MRMC (1922), 35.
172. Ibid.
173. Ibid. (1924), 60.
174. ECAMC (1901), 13.
175. Ibid., 14.
176. Ibid.
177. Ibid. (1915), 46.
178. MRMCMEC (3–10 May 1917), 6.
179. MRMC (1917), 6.
180. MRMC (1919), 39.
181. Ibid.
182. Ibid.
183. Ibid. (1917), 50.
184. Ibid., 49.
185. ECAMC (1905), 24.
186. MRMC (1925), 54.
187. Ibid.
188. Edward Krusen Ziegler, *The Village Pastor* (New York: Agricultural Missions, Inc., 1959), 71.
189. Ibid., 70.
190. Ibid., 12.
191. Bart D. Ehrman, *The New Testament* (Oxford: Oxford University Press, 2000), 277.
192. Edward Krusen Ziegler, *The Village Pastor* (New York: Agricultural Missions, Inc. 1959), 54.
193. *Webster's New World Dictionary*, 1247.
194. Samuel Dzobo, "A History and Theology of Evangelism: An Assessment of How Both Clergy and Laity Leadership Contributes to the Ministry," unpublished dissertation, Africa University (2006), 83.
195. Ibid., 84.
196. MRMC (1919), 26.

197. Ibid., 28.
198. Ibid., 37.
199. MRMC (1924), 35. Janson Machiwenyika, *History of the Manyika People,* trans. W. S. Musewe in 1943 (an unpublished manuscript in MA 14/1/2, National Archives). Janson Machiwenyika was a teacher, and well known in the conference of The Methodist Episcopal Church for being conversant with African customs and the history of the Manyika people. By the time of his death in 1924, he had accumulated hundreds of pages of history and folklore stories that he had written.
200. MRMC (1919), 26.
201. Ibid., 58.
202. Ibid., 37.
203. Ibid.
204. Ibid., 46._
205. Ibid., 28.
206. Ibid., 55.
207. Ibid., 32.
208. "The Mission Extension of the United Methodist Church in Africa," *Umbowo* (October 1972), 5.
209. MRMC (1921), 49.
210. "The Mission Extension of The Methodist Church in Africa (1816–1896), *Umbowo* (Dec. 1972), 37.
211. MRMC (1921), 11.
212. Ibid. (1926), 18.
213. Ibid. (1927), 20.
214. Ibid. (1928), 19.
215. Ibid. (1929), 19.
216. Barclay M. Newman, Jr., *A Concise Greek-English Dictionary of the New Testament*. (London: United Bible Societies, 1971), 42.
217. Ibid.
218. *The Christian as Minister* (1997), 39.
219. Ibid., 10.
220. Ibid., 12.
221. G. S. P. Freeman-Grenville, *The New Atlas of African History* (New York: Simon & Schuster, 1991), 23.
222. Ibid., 10.
223. Faculty of Health Sciences: Africa University.
224. Ibid.
225. Henry H. Mitchell, *The Recovery of Preaching* (San Francisco: Harper & Row, 1977), 6–7.
226. Eugen Rosenstock-Huessy, *Out of Revolution* (Norwich, Vt.: Argo Books, 1969), 524.